THE AMERICAN FLAG IS THE REAL SLAVE FLAG

by
Stanley K. Lott

SKL Publications
Passaic, New Jersey

The American Flag is the Real Slave Flag
by Stanley K. Lott

Third Edition
Copyright © 2005, 2015 by Stanley K. Lott

Published by SKL Publications
343 Oak Street #1 Passaic, New Jersey 07055

Cover and Interior by Magnolia Graphic Design
www.magnoliagraphicdesign.com

ISBN-13: 978-0692425671
ISBN-10: 0692425675

CONTENTS

❖ ◆ ❖

FOREWORD
by Dr. Robert Brock
The World's Authority on the United States Constitution and the African Slave

◆ ◆ ◆

Slave Clauses in the U.S. Constitution;
The U.S. Constitution Protected Slavery

In a descending order, the following writings herein show a negation of mutuality and consent.

The Fourteenth Amendment, the largest adhesion contract in the world, is forced on Blacks of U.S. slave descent.

The Dred Scott Decision, 19 Howard 393 (1857) was forced on Blacks of U.S. slave descent.

The Constitution for the United States of America (1787) was forced onto Blacks with the following slave clauses (see Appendix).

The territorial jurisdiction, laws, statutes, rules, and regulations were forced on Blacks of U.S. slave descent.

The Sixteenth Amendment tax codes and regulations and the Internal Revenue Service are presently forced on U.S. slave descendants without due process.

INTRODUCTION

◆ ◆ ◆

My name is Stanley K. Lott. I was born and raised in Saluda, South Carolina. I am a Black Southern American. My reason for writing this book is to help people understand the role the U.S. Government played in supporting and sustaining American slavery and the slave trade. Since I have found out the real truth about slavery and slave trade, I feel some relief. A Black person does not need excess emotional baggage or garbage in their lives. Slavery was well protected by the Constitution of the United States, the U.S. Federal Government, the Supreme Court, and the American flag. At home it was protected by the American flag, and at sea under international law and the laws of nations. So someone might say to themselves, Why has the truth about slavery not been told or why has it been diluted? I might have the answer: The more ignorant the elites of this society (communist and socialist people) keep the masses, the easier it is for them to pull their tricks and maneuvers.

Special interest groups play the race card. They play Black people against White people, Northerners against Southerners, and Jews against Gentiles. That is why a good education is important, not just a mental education (book learning), but a spiritual education. People need to have standards and principles to stand up for when they know it is the truth. We need men like John C. Calhoun around today to stand up and help to keep the U.S. Government in its official boundaries.

    I want to thank men like Dr. Walter Williams, Thomas Sowell, and Clarence Thomas (even though I have some reservations about his thinking on affirmative action). Thomas did make a good life for himself by going to college and getting appointed to the U.S. Supreme Court. Let me go on to thank men like Thomas DiLorenzo, Lorene Bennett Jr., Charles Adams, and Walter D. and James R. Kennedy. They have written some good books and articles that have increased my knowledge about slavery, taxes, States' rights, etc. Now here are some things that people can look up on the Internet to see how the U.S. Government supported and protected slavery:

Crittenden Compromise

The Corwin Amendment

President Abraham Lincoln proposed
the Thirteenth Amendment

President Abraham Lincol''s first Inaugural Address

S.R. 70 – Passed on February 28, 1861
by the Thirty-Sixth Congress, second Session

The Fugitive Slave Laws (of 1793 and 1850)

PREFACE

◆ ◆ ◆

The contents of this book is very sensitive material. I, the writer, Stanley K. Lott, take all responsibility for what I have written. I can prove what I say in this book before any special interest groups. This book is not written to defame or embarrass the United States Government or anybody, but to tell the truth about U.S. history and slavery. This kind of truth some people might want to keep secret, but I think it should be made known. I advise anyone (Black or White) who reads this book to obey and honor the laws of the United States. The times and events spoken of in this book are in the past. Understand it and accept things properly. Please control your feelings and leave the past in the past. Let us all work together to make the United States a better and safer place in which to live. Thank you for buying and reading my book.

Stanley K. Lott
independent researcher and writer

ACKNOWLEDGMENTS

◆   ◆   ◆

I wish to give thanks to the Huddle House staff in Saluda, South Carolina – Ms. Suzanne Long and Gwen, along with the others. They were the people who encouraged me to write a book. I want to give thanks to all the people who helped me in my time of need. I want to thank men like Dr. Michael Hill, H. K. Edgerton, Dr. Walter Williams, Bob Harrison, and others who knew the true U. S. History and stood up for it. I also wish to thank Clarence Thomas, Armstrong Williams, Sowell Thomas, and other Blacks who have shown that working hard and getting a good education is the right thing to do. Finally, I wish to thank Dr. Robert Brock for allowing me to include his "Slave Clauses in the U. S. Constitution" (see Appendix).

CHAPTER ONE
The American Flag is the Real Slave Flag

◆ ◆ ◆

To begin, I want to talk about the American flag. But for now, let me explain to you, the reader, about flags. When you see, for example, the United Nations building in New York City with the United Nations flag, it shows that the jurisdiction you are in or looking at belongs to the United Nations and not the United States. Even though the place is physically located in the United States, you are under the jurisdiction of the United Nations the moment you step foot on their grounds. You are subject to their rules, regulations, and penalties if you commit a crime or offense while you are on that property.

It is the same with the embassies of different countries. If it is an official government building of another country that you are entering, please take the time to find out their rules and regulations or stay off the grounds. A flag flown in an official capacity implies the jurisdiction of the country whose flag it is.

Now, let us go to the ships at sea. I'm going to explain this the best I can. I am not an expert in international law, but this I do know – if you see a ship at sea flying the French flag, the ship is under the rules and regulations of that country (France). If an American boards that ship in the middle of the Atlantic Ocean (this is just an example) and commits a crime, he will be prosecuted under the laws of that nation (France). Even though he was on that ship in the middle of the Atlantic Ocean when he committed that crime, he was under the jurisdiction of France. Please remember a flag flown on an official government building or ship implies the jurisdiction it is under.

Now let us speak of slaves (and passengers at sea). For example, you and I are at sea on an American ship flying the American flag. A British ship pulls up beside our ship. They kidnap or take us as hostages, and rob us of our goods and money. Under international law, they have committed crimes against the United States of America (and its American citizens). The United States can demand that retribution and justice be done. Great Britain would have to answer to the United States and make sure punishment gets issued and justice is done. Now I hope you have some idea of how passengers and merchandise at sea are protected under international law. (Reference: See "Treaty of Washington"). Here is the first example of how slaves were protected at sea under the American flag. Please read it for yourself, in direct quotes, following this.

Direct Quotes

This was taken directly from the *Congressional Globe,* Thirty-sixth Congress, Second Session:

The Constitution was adapted to the institution of slavery as it then existed and was in accordance with the public sentiment of the whole country at the time. Accordingly, no man doubted that it recognized PROPERTY IN SLAVES and was designed to PROTECT IT WHEREVER THE NATIONAL FLAG WAS UNFURLED

ON SEA OR ON LAND. No question was made as to the right of the master to carry his slave with him into the common territories of the Union.

Even the men of Massachusetts would no doubt have conceded it: Its denial would have lessened the market consequently depreciated the price that the New England slave trader might get for the slaves he was importing by the shipload. The FLAG OF THE UNION [American flag] PROTECTED THIS PROPERTY on its passage from Africa to slave States of the South. The treaties of the country with foreign nations specially stipulated for the indemnification of the loss of slaves. This was done by Jay's treaty. It was done in the treaty of Ghent and the treaty of acquisition of Louisiana recognizes and protects the right of property in slaves (*Congressional Globe,* Thirty-Sixth Congress, Second Session, page 357, middle column).

Over every sea the American flag will still wave; not "the ensign of one of the little North American Republics," but as the flag of the United States, feared for the power whose symbol it is, honored by a thousand recollections, endeared by a thousand associations, and perhaps, not less glorious in the sight of the civilized world when SLAVERY SHALL HAVE CEASED TO RECOGNIZE THAT BANNER AS ITS EMBLEM (page 552, left column).

I seem, sir, to have been listening, for two months past, to powerful efforts of argument and oratory on all sides of this house, and in the other branch of Congress to satisfy the country that the extension of slavery in the territories, and its PROTECTION EVERY-WHERE UNDER THE AUTHORITY OF THE NATIONAL FLAG, was the first and paramount constitutional duty of the United States Government (Appendix, page 1008, End of middle and top of right column).

Sir, the proposition known as the "Border States Compromise" which is similar to that of the Gentlemen from Illinois (Mr. Kellogg) if I understand it, is scarcely less objectionable. It provides that the Constitution shall be amended that, in all territory south of 36° 30', neither Congress nor the people of the territory shall ever interfere with or prohibit slavery. This is as effectual PROTECTION TO SLAVERY as though it were provided for in express terms. It is only another way of reaching the same result (page 760, right column).

Sir, the Union is dear to the people of the Northern States; they would sacrifice much to preserve it as it is. But a Union FOUNDED ON THE PROTECTION OF SLAVERY, as its "Chief Cornerstone Stone," is not the Union for which our fathers fought, and is not the precious boon which they supposed they had transmitted to their prosperity. If the only terms upon which the Union can be preserved are, that the General Government, by constitutional provision and congressional enactment, shall through all time, wherever the adventurous spirit of our people shall plant the AMERICAN BANNER [flag] be pledged to the protection of an institution [slavery] condemned by the whole civilized world, outside of the slave States – an institution which Mr. Hunter, in his speech in Charlottesville, in August last, said that "SOUTHERN MEN THEMSELVES, WITH BUT FEW EXCEPTIONS, ADMITTED TO BE A MORAL EVIL," not twenty years ago – then, indeed, will the North begin to "calculate the value" of such a Union (page 760, right column).

Could anything be more explicit than the assertion of the right to protection of property everywhere, wherever the FEDERAL FLAG floats or the federal government has jurisdiction. "That it is the duty of the Fed eral Government in all its departments, to protect, when necessary, the rights of persons and property in the territories, and wherever else its constitutional authority extends." Both upon the land and upon the sea, it is the duty of the Federal Government to protect property of every species, SLAVES AS WELL AS OTHER PROPERTY (page 787, bottom of middle column).

Mr. Breckinridge ran as a candidate for the presidency upon a platform which declared explicitly that SLAVES WERE PROPERTY, and like all other property, were ENTITLED TO PROTECTION WHEREVER THE FEDERAL FLAG FLOATED, wherever the Federal Government has jurisdiction (Appendix, page 1373).

The proposition known as the Crittenden Compromise declares not only that "in the territory south of the said Line of Latitude, SLAVERY OF THE AFRICAN RACE is hereby recognized as existing, and SHALL NOT BE INTERFERED WITH BY THE CONGRESS;" but it provides further, that, in the territory we shall hereafter acquire south of that line, slavery shall be recognized, and not interfered with by Congress, but "shall be protected as property by all the departments of the territorial government during its continuance;" so that, if we make acquisitions on the south of the territories now free, and whereby the laws of the land, the footsteps of slavery have never been, the moment we acquire jurisdiction over them, the moment the Stars and Stripes of the republic float over those free territories, they carry with them AFRICAN SLAVERY, established beyond the power of Congress and beyond the power of any Territorial Legislature or the people, to keep it out (Appendix, page 1381).

The doctrine that slavery only exists by positive law means, that when the slave is carried beyond the jurisdiction of a State which sanctions and authorizes slavery by its positive law, he becomes entitled to his freedom. If then the Federal Government does not recognize the right of PROPERTY IN SLAVES, what becomes of the property in a slave when, under the FEDERAL FLAG, the vessel [ship] is more than a marine league from the shore? There is no State jurisdiction, there is no authority to keep him in bondage, if the principle be sound that the moment he gets beyond the jurisdiction of a State which sanctions slavery, he is entitled to his freedom, unless the Federal Government recognizes the right of the property in a slave (page 1486, top middle column).

The Supreme Court of the United States has decided that the Constitution recognizes slavery: that Congress has neither power to prohibit or establish it, but as it is BOUND to the extent of its jurisdiction to PROTECT SLAVE PROPERTY as it does any other species of property which is recognized as property in the States existing under a common Government (page 1486, left column, past halfway down column).

When the State of Kentucky came into this Union of States, slavery was prohibited, not only by statute, but also by constitution; by compact irrepealable, in every inch of territory over which Federal jurisdiction was exerted. When, in 1789, George Washington took the oath to support the Constitution of the United States, the FEDERAL FLAG did not wave over an inch of this broad earth, outside of the limits of a State, where slavery was not prohibited in the most solemn forms of a compact declared to be irrepealable (page 1469, right column).

You have got now a judicial exposition of the Constitution by the highest judicial tribunal of the land, that slavery extends, by virtue of the Constitution, WHEREVER THE JURISDICTION OF THE CONSTITUTION GOES, and that all the power that Congress has over the subject is the power, coupled with the duty, of the power, coupled with the duty, of PROTECTION (page 1469, right column).

You have got the territory in all its length and breadth, North and South, East and West, and we have none to give unless we give up to you that strip of sea-shore that we own, extending three miles from the coast; for I believe that is the only place where the FEDERAL FLAG waves outside of a State, where you have not got everything that you ever claimed for slavery (March 18, 1861, page 1470, bottom of left column).

They should distinctly understand, that while the people of the FREE STATES [Northern States] ARE INVOLVED IN THE SUPPORT OF SLAVERY in this district, or the coast-wise slave trade; while Congress lends its powers and influence to rob a portion of the people of their inalienable rights, Northern philanthropy and Northern patriotism will make their voices heard in this hall; nor will they be silenced until this District is rendered free, until the NATION'S FLAG shall cease to float over the CARGOES OF SLAVES and the territories of the United States shall be exempt from the curse of oppression (*Congressional* Globe, Appendix, Thirtieth Congress, second session, House of Representatives, page 128).

Think what could be effected by the Federal legislation. Abolition of slavery in the District of Columbia, abolition in the arsenals, dockyards, and forts; outlawry of it on the high seas, and wherever the FLAG OF THE UNION floats; exclusion of it from the common territories belonging equally to all the States; circumscribing it as with a wall of fire within the States (*Congressional Globe,* Appendix, Thirtieth Congress, Second Session, page 357, middle column). (This shows that the American flag, not the Confederate flag, flew over slavery).

New York City and Slave Ships

Mr. Morse, I shall oppose and vote against this amendment, because I propose to offer an amendment to this section, the object of which will be to apply a portion of this $2,500,000 to the purchase of six good, fast going steamers, suitable for service on the coast of Africa, and to be sent immediately to that coast for the prevention of the AFRICAN SLAVE TRADE.

There is another reason why we should purchase instead of build. The demand for immediate action is strong and urgent. Vessels for the slave trade are almost continually preparing for the horrid and inhuman traffic in several of our leading Atlantic ports [especially in the port of New York City].

Here is an opportunity for action, for showing the country and mankind that we are seriously in earnest, and mean to put an end to lawless traffic now carried on UNDER THE AMERICAN FLAG in open violations of our laws and the rights of man.

Because the President of the United States had communicated to us a document showing that, to an atrocious and nefarious extent, the slave trade was carried on under the American Flag from the coast of Brazil to the western coast of Africa. I called the attention of the Senate to the fact and moved a resolution to instruct the committee to inquire into and report on the subject. (Appendix to the *Congressional Globe*, Thirty-first Congress, second session, Senate, Titled "Fugitive Slave Law," Messrs Chase and Clay, Page 322).

All twelve of the following quotes are from the same reference.

All importations of slaves into any of the States that existed at the adoption of the Constitution was prohibited after 1808: but by additional encouragement and facilities which the business receiving generally at the

hand of the Government, State and Federal, have PROS-
TITUTED OUR FLAG ABROAD TO ENGAGE IN THE
AFRICAN SLAVE TRADE.

Sir, I am mortified to learn by reference to their
correspondence that my predecessors have been com-
pelled to report to your department frequent instances of
the use of THE FLAG OF OUR COUNTRY IN THE INFA-
MOUS TRAFFIC OF CARRYING NEGROES [slaves]
from the coast of Africa to Brazil. It has also been their
painful duty to announce the fact of American citizens
being engaged in this abominable trade. I deeply regret
that it is likewise incumbent upon me to address my
Government upon the subject.

This [slave] traffic should, at all hazards, be put
down; and when I inform you that by far the greater
portion of it is carried on in vessels built in the United
States and UNDER THE AMERICAN FLAG, I trust you
will agree with me that it becomes us to act and to act
promptly. For myself, I will do so with a very good will.

The fact that the American ship, *Senator*, proceeded to the coast of Africa, in the month of December
last, and brought to the coast of Brazil a large cargo of
NEGRO SLAVES. The deposition (an abstract of which
I give to you marked A) represents a scene of cruelty
and horror indescribable. It will be difficult, if not impossible, wholly to rescue the American vessels and the
AMERICAN FLAG from this SLAVE TRADE.

We build better ships and at less cost in the
United States, than are built in any other part of the
world. The SLAVE TRADER finds it to be to his inter-
ests to use American vessels. But above all, the AMERI-
CAN FLAG gives to vessels throughout the world a protection that is afforded by no other flag.

This proof establishes beyond question the fact that the American ship *Senator*, under the AMERICAN FLAG, sailed from this harbor in the month of December last, to the coast of Africa for a CARGO OF SLAVES. She received on board some nine hundred blacks and that after a short voyage, she returned and landed in Macahi, a Brazilian port city.

Fifty thousand Africans are annually imported into Brazil and SOLD AS SLAVES FOR LIFE. I believe one half of this number are introduced through the facilities, directly and indirectly afforded by the AMERICAN FLAG.

I regret to say this, but it is a fact not to be so disguised or denied, that the SLAVE TRADE is almost entirely carried on under the AMERICAN FLAG.

The AMERICAN FLAG alone gives the requisite protections against the right of visit, search, and seizure; and our citizens, in all the characters of owners, consignees, agents, masters, and crews of our vessels, are concerned in this business. We partake of these profits of the AFRICAN SLAVE TRADE to and from the ports of Brazil.

Here is the testimony of Mr. Profit and Mr. Wise. Both concur in the same statement made by Mr. Tod: That under the AMERICAN FLAG, with American seamen, and with full knowledge of the United States Government is the wretched, humiliating AFRICAN SLAVE TRADE carried on, at the rate of twenty-five to fifty thousand a year. These facts have been pressed upon the United States Government from year to year since 1844 until the present time, unheeded.

In this equal struggle between humanity and patriotism on the one hand, and cupidity and self-interest on the other, the influence of the AMERICAN FLAG is scarcely felt, except IN SUPPORT OF THE SLAVE DEALER. The seizures made by American men-of-war weighing as nothing in the scale with facilities which OUR COLORS [the American flag] afford in the transportation to Africa of slave goods, slave crews, and slave vessels.

Shall it be said to our everlasting shame and disgrace that OUR FLAG, the most honored and admired flag in the whole wide world has prostituted its honor and pride in the sordid LUST OF SLAVERY, to the extent that it can calmly look on and see with silent approbation forty thousand citizens of Africa torn from home, country, and friends. They are tumbled into holds of the ship and taken to market. Then they are sold, living or dying, to the highest bidder.

These excerpts are taken from the Appendix to the *Congressional Globe*, Thirty-second Congress, First Session, titled "Fugitive Slave Law," House of Representatives, page 971, year 1852.

CHAPTER TWO
Continuation of States Rights

◆ ◆ ◆

This is a good example of the principles of States' rights. The people of the States have reserved to themselves certain powers and certain rights (see Ninth and Tenth Amendments to the U.S. Constitution), limited and defined only by their will, so long as they do not interfere with the powers invested in Congress. By these reserved powers, in accordance with these reserved rights, certain States recognized property in slaves. The Constitution guaranteed protection to this property under certain circumstances and the Congress of the United States, by virtue of its constitutional obligation, was bound to execute this guarantee. This was one of the conditions of our political compact and no State was bound by it, politically or morally, any longer than the constitutional guarantee for the protection of life and property was faithfully carried out. And what was the fugitive slave law but a law to execute this guarantee? I think this was a show of respect for the different boundaries of the States and Federal Government. When one over-steps its boundaries, there is a conflict of interest. If we the people of the United States could have this kind of respect today, what a country this would be.

Now let us go on and talk about another quote that shows respect and harmony among the different States. Here it is, taken directly from the Appendix to the *Congressional Globe*, Thirty-second Congress, First Session, titled "The Fugitive Slave Law," Mr. Sumner, page 1106. This shows States working together for a common goal and having mutual respect for each other's rights, even though the South made threats. It takes some madness sometimes to get what you need to have.

> There was a compromise between the small and large States, by which equality was secured to all the States in the Senate. There was another compromise finally carried under the threats from the South, on the motion of a New England member by which the slave States were allowed representatives according to the whole number of free persons and "three fifths of all other persons," thus securing political power on account of their slaves in consideration that direct taxes should be apportioned in the same way. Direct taxes have been imposed at only four brief intervals. The political power has been constant and at this moment sends twenty-one members to the other House.

Looking at another example of States' rights, one will see how it may not always work in people's favor. Here it is taken directly from the Appendix to the *Congressional Globe*, Thirty-second Congress, First Session, page 1109, Year 1852:

> The same principle of States rights, by which slavery is protected in the slave States, throws its impenetrable shield over freedom in the free States. Here let me say it is the only security for slavery in the slave States, as for free men in the free States. In the present fatal overthrow of States rights, you teach a lesson which may return to plague the teacher. Compelling the Nation-

al Government to stretch its Briarean arms into the free States for the sake of slavery, *you show how openly it may stretch these same hundred giant arms into the slave States for the sake of freedom.* This lesson was not taught by our Fathers.

This did happen after the Civil War when the ratified Thirteenth Amendment was passed in December of 1865 to end slavery in the United States. Also, President Abraham Lincoln and his Civil War destroyed the real power of States rights and State sovereignty. He also violated the U. S. Constitution that he swore an oath to uphold.

Here is something to show how the relationship between the States and the Federal Government is supposed to be:

That the several States composing the United States of America are not united upon the principle of unlimited submission to the General Government: but that by compact under the style and title of the Constitution of the United States, they constituted a General Government for special purposes. They delegated to that Government certain definite powers, reserving to each State the powers not delegated to the Federal Government. Whenever the Federal Government assumes undelegated powers, the acts are unauthorized, void, and of no force.

This shows that the integrity of our political system depends upon harmony in the operations of the National and State governments. While the National Government, within its wide orbit, is supreme, the State governments move with equal supremacy in their own orbit. From the necessity of the case of supremacy, each in its proper place excludes the other. The Federal Government cannot exercise rights reserved to the States; nor can the States interfere with the powers of the National Government. Any such action on either side is a usurpation. These principles were distinctly declared by Mr. Jefferson in 1798 (reference: Appendix to the *Congressional Globe*, Thirty-second Congress, First Session, "The Fugitive Slave Law," Senate, page 1109, year 1852).

Here is another example of States' rights and State sovereignty taken from the *Congressional Globe*, Thirty-sixth Congress, Second Session, page 293, year 1861. It says:

Mr President, this is not the time to discuss the principles of Government. I do not regard this Government as a great consolidated Government. This is not a Federal Government in which State lines are not known or State sovereignty is not regarded. The other day when the Senator from Oregon (Mr. Baker) was on the floor, he took the occasion to speak of this Government as a great consolidated Government in which the States were not known as such, or the sovereignty of States was not considered when entitling them to rights, if I understood them right, but I have not read his speech. The idea was that the States had no rights secured to them! It was a great Government in itself without reference to State boundaries or State sovereignty. Now sir, I took the occasion to look over the Constitution a little afterward, and I found in the nineteen articles of the Constitution, including the amendments, that States are specially mentioned over thirty times. Because State sovereignty is recognized that many times and that States are referred to, I think any man who has examined the question will say that this is a Government of the States, a Confederation of States, a voluntary association of States, and as the Senator from Ohio (Mr. Pugh) so handsomely said: The Atlas upon which this Union rests is the sovereignty of the States, each of them having equal rights in the United States. Respect them as such, regard them as such, maintain the perfect equality, maintain justice, and deal fairly by every person of every State of the United States. Recognize every State alike, and peace can be restored without a passage of this bill. It is hardly the time to pass such a measure.

The bill was a measure to award the South $36,000,000 because their rights had been violated. From what I have read, this would have been an insult to their principles and integrity.

A Supreme Court Case That Supported States' Rights and State Sovereignty

In *Groves vs. Slaughter*, the argument urged was that by the Constitution of the United States, the regulation of the trade between the States and consequently the regulation of the trade in slaves between the States was vested in the Congress of the United States, and that no State can undertake to prohibit within its own borders the introduction of slaves, they being an article of commerce, from other States. The State of Mississippi had provided that by her constitution, slaves should not be introduced within her limits as merchandise. The argument of the counsel was that it was a power which belonged to Congress and not to the State of Mississippi.

The court decided that it was a power which every State had a right to exercise, and that every State in the United States might forbid the introduction of slaves within her limits as merchandise from any of the other States. That was the decision of the Supreme Court and that decision is the only matter of any consequence in the consideration of this question.

CHAPTER THREE
The African Slave Trade

◆   ◆   ◆

Resolved, that the Committee on Foreign Relations be instructed to inquire into the expediency of providing by law for such restrictions on the power of American consuls residing in the Spanish West India Islands to issue sea letters on the transfer of American vessels in those islands, as will prevent the abuse of the AMERICAN FLAG in protecting persons engaged in the AFRICAN SLAVE TRADE (*Journal of the Senate*, May 22, 1854, Thirty-third Congress, First Session, Volume 45, page 404).

Your committee finds it impossible to measure with precision the effect produced upon the AMERICAN BRANCH OF THE SLAVE TRADE by the laws above mentioned and the seizures under them. They are unable to state whether those American merchants, the American capital, and seamen which heretofore aided in this traffic, have abandoned it altogether, or have sought shelter under the flags of other nations. It is ascertained, however, that the AMERICAN FLAG, which heretofore covered a large portion of the SLAVE TRADE, has wholly disappeared from the cost of Africa (Seventeenth Congress, First Session, "Suppression of the Slave Trade," pages 140, 351).

Communicated to the House of Representatives, April 12, 1822.

The suppression of the AFRICAN SLAVE TRADE has received the continued attention of the government. The brig, *Dolphin*, and the schooner, *Grampus*, have been employed during the last season on the coast of Africa, for the purpose of preventing such portions of that trade as was said to be prosecuted under the AMERICAN FLAG. After cruising off the coast most usually resorted to by slavers, until the commencement of the rainy season, these vessels returned to the United States for supplies, and have since been dispatched on a similar service (*Journal of the House of Representatives*, Twenty-sixth Congress, Second Session, Wednesday, December 9, 1840, page 24).

From the reports of the commanding officers, it appears that the [AFRICAN SLAVE] TRADE is now principally carried on under Portuguese colors; and they express the opinion that the apprehension of their presence on the slave coast, has in great degree, arrested the prostitution of the AMERICAN FLAG to this inhumane purpose. It is hoped that, by continuing to maintain this force in that quarter, and by the exertions of the officers in command, much will be done to put a stop to whatever portion of this traffic may have been carried on under the AMERICAN FLAG and to prevent its use in a trade which, while it violates the laws, is equally an outrage on the rights of others and the feelings of humanity.

Congress never ought, and I trust never will, plant the standard [flag] of the Union in Missouri, to wave over the heads of involuntary slaves, who have nothing they can call their own, except their sorrows and sufferings (*Journal of the Senate*, December 9, 1820, Saturday, Sixteenth Congress, Second Session, page 53).

The Senate proceeded to consider the resolution,

submitted by Mr. Archer the 20th instant, relating to the use of the AMERICAN FLAG in subservience to the AFRICAN SLAVE TRADE: and the resolution was agreed to (*Journal of the Senate*, Wednesday, February 21, 1844, page 131).

Due attention has likewise been paid to the suppression of the SLAVE TRADE, in compliance with a law of that last session. Orders have been given to the commanders of all public ships to seize all vessels navigated under our flag [AMERICAN FLAG], engaged in that trade and to bring them in, to be proceeded against, in the manner prescribed by the law (*Journal of the House of Representatives*, Tuesday, December 7, 1819, page 19).

The usual orders have been given to all our public ships to seize American vessels engaged in the SLAVE TRADE, and bring them in for adjudication, and I have the gratification to state, that not one so employed has been discovered, and there is good reason to believe our flag [AMERICAN FLAG] is seldom, if at all disgraced by that traffic (*Journal of the Senate*, December 2, 1823, Tuesday, page 17).

Resolved, that the President of the United States, if in his opinion it shall be not incompatible with the public interest, be requested to communicate to the Senate any correspondence which may have passed between Her Britannic Majesty government and the minister of the United States in London, of a recent date, touching the abuses of the AMERICAN FLAG in the prosecution [carrying on] of the AFRICAN SLAVE TRADE on the coast of Africa, and especially touching the cruise of the *Wanderer* on that coast (*Journal of the Senate*, Friday, January 7, 1859, page 115).

Resolved, that the President be requested to communicate to Congress, as far as he considers consistent with the public interest, any information, which may have reached the government, from its accredited agents, tending to show any use of the FLAG OF THE UNITED STATES in subservience to the AFRICAN SLAVE TRADE and in violation of the laws or policies of the government; also, any correspondence which may have taken place between this government and the minister of Portugal subjects, from the territories of that power, in vessels owned or employed by citizens of the United States (*Journal of the Senate*, February 20, 1844, Tuesday, page 127).

The AFRICAN SLAVE TRADE has, it is believed, been entirely suppressed in Brazil, and in this hemisphere – the remaining colonies of Spain, Cuba, and Port Rico – are its only mart. Your committee thinks that if the AMERICAN FLAG be still employed in this nefarious traffic now prohibited in every Christian nation and surreptitiously tolerated by Spain alone, the abuse can be more effectively corrected by the employment of our cruisers in the vicinity of those islands. Ordered, that it be printed in confidence for the use of the Senate (*Senate Executive Journal*, June 19, 1854, Thirty-third Congress, First Session, Monday, page 336).

These objects during the present year, have been accomplished more effectively than at any other period. The AFRICAN SLAVE TRADE has long been excluded from the use of our flag [AMERICAN FLAG] (*Journal of the House of Representatives*, Tuesday, December 6, 1825, Page 20).

Eminence in the SLAVE TRADE has long disgracefully distinguished a number of the citizens of an Eastern State. Regardless of their own and their country's reputation, they have long been inhumane forgers of chains for the sons of Africa. By their means the

AMERICAN FLAG still continues to flutter over an insulted territory, the witness of the greatest enormities. Parents are torn from children, husbands from wives; in a word, thousands of free men are annually dragged into slavery, through the instrumentality of the vessels, the citizens, and the produce of the United States; and this, too, in undisguised contravention of the laws of their country (*Annuals of Congress*, Senate, Ninth Congress, Second Session).

Resolved, that so much of the message of the President of the United States, as relates to commercial abuse committed under the AMERICAN FLAG, in carrying on an illegal traffic in enslaved Africans [SLAVE TRADE], be referred to a committee to examine and report thereon to the Senate: and that the committee have leave to report by bill or otherwise (*Journal of the Senate*, Year 1810, page 527).

Among the commercial abuses still committed under the AMERICAN FLAG, and leaving in force my former reference to the subject, it appears that American citizens are instrumental in carrying on a TRAFFIC IN ENSLAVED AFRICANS, equally in violation of the laws of humanity and in defiance of those of their own country (House of Representatives, Year 1810, page 435).

Such were my views at the time of negotiating that treaty, and such, in my opinion, is its plain and fair interpretation. I regarded the eighth article as removing all possible pretext, on the ground of mere necessity, to visit and detain our ships upon the African coast because of any alleged abuse of our flag [AMERICAN FLAG] by SLAVE TRADERS of other nations (House of Representatives, Tuesday, February 28, 1843, page 487).

Resolved, that the President of the United States, if in his opinion it shall be not incompatible with the public interest, be requested to communicate to the Senate any correspondence which may have been passed between Her Britannic Majesty's government and the minister of the United States in London of a recent date, touching the abuses of the AMERICAN FLAG in the prosecution of the AFRICAN SLAVE TRADE on the coast of Africa, and especially touching the cruise of the *Wanderer* on that coast (*Journal of the Senate*, Friday, January 7, 1859, page 115).

1. Resolved, that it will be expedient to raise an additional revenue of two million dollars, annually, by a direct tax.
2. Resolved, that the said tax ought to be laid, by uniform assessment, on lands, houses, and SLAVES (House of Representatives, Saturday, May 5, 1798).

Resolved, that a tax or duty of ten dollars per head, be imposed upon all SLAVES hereafter IMPOR- TED into any of the United States (House of Representatives, Wednesday, December 11, 1805, page 195).

The speaker also laid before the House a letter from the Secretary of the Treasury, to which is annexed a statement of the valuation of lands, lots, and dwelling houses, and SLAVES, made under the act laying a direct tax, in pursuance of the resolution of the 8th instant; which was read and ordered to lie on the table (House of Representatives, February 15, 1816, page 349).

On the question, that the House do agree to the last part of the said resolution, in the words following, to wit: "A tax on SLAVES, with certain exceptions (*Journal of the House of Representatives*, Year 1797, page 652).

An engrossed bill, for imposing a tax of ten dol- lars on all SLAVES hereafter IMPORTED into the United

States (House of Representatives, February 27, 1806, page 305).

A petition of Jacob Greer, of the State of North Carolina, was presented to the House and read, paying compensation for services rendered, and expenses incurred; by the petitioner in completing the collection of the tax on lands, dwelling houses, and SLAVES for the thirty-ninth collection district, composed of the county of Orange, in the State of North Carolina (House of Representatives, Wednesday, January 30, 1805, page 112).

Resolved, that a tax of ten dollars be imposed on EVERY SLAVE IMPORTED into any part of the United States (House of Representatives, Monday, January 9, 1804).

Resolved, that a tax of ten dollars be imposed on every SLAVE IMPORTED into any part of the United States, or their territories (House of Representatives, Wednesday, February 15, 1804, page 580).

The House, according to the order of the day, again resolved itself a committee of the whole house on a motion of the tenth of December last, "To impose a tax or duty of ten dollars per head upon all SLAVES hereafter IMPORTED into any of the United States" (House of Representatives, January 21, 1806, page 242).

The House, according to the order of the day, again resolved itself into a committee of the whole house on a motion of the tenth ultimo, "to impose a tax or duty of ten dollars per head upon all SLAVES hereafter IMPORTED into any of the Unites States (House of Representatives, Wednesday, January 22, 1806, page 243).

Mr. Stuart presented a petition of John R. Plafer, of Maryland, praying to be exonerated from the payment of the tax lately levied on his SLAVES under the act of imposing a direct tax, as his SLAVES have been subsequently stolen from him by the enemy (House of Representatives, Tuesday, November 8, 1814, page 519).

CHAPTER FOUR
Protection of Slavery by the
U.S. Government

◆ ◆ ◆

What would most people say if a person told them that the U. S. Government, the U. S. Constitution, the Supreme Court, and the American flag protected, sanctioned, supported, and sustained American slavery? Someone in this politically correct world most likely would say you are lying. They would probably also think anyone who thought something like that was insane. But here is some proof. This is taken directly from the *Congressional Globe* (Thirty-sixth Congress, Second Session, page 357, middle column). The Constitution of the United States was designed to protect slavery wherever the national flag was flying at sea or on land (a flag in this instance would imply jurisdiction – American jurisdiction). The article goes on to further state that no question was made as to the right of a master to carry his slave with him into the common territories of the Union (United States). Even the men of Massachusetts would no doubt have conceded it. Its denial would have lessened the market and consequently depreciated the price that the New England slave trader might get for the slaves he was importing from Africa by ship. This helps to prove what Abraham Lincoln said about the North being just as responsible for slavery as the South. If it were not for slaves being transported to this country in British, Dutch, and New England owned slave ships, most of them probably would not have gotten to the United States.

To get to the root of slavery (the origin of power and domination in the slave trade) might disturb some people. But it is a situation that needs to be addressed in this present day and time, not only to relieve Southern White people of guilt but to relieve Black people of anger and madness. Southern White people did not have to fight to protect something (slavery) that was already protected by the U. S. Government, the Supreme Court, and the American flag. Because so many lies, myths, and half-truths have been told about the Civil War and the Confederate battle flag that is a shame. Some of what is written in American history books is lies and distortions.

As I continue to prove that slavery was well protected by our own Government, please do not think that I'm anti-American. I'm just telling the truth about human bondage. Our own Constitution states in Article IV, Section 2, Clause 3, that "No person held to service or labor, escaping to another State, shall be discharged from that service or labor, but shall be delivered up, upon claim to such person to whom such service is due." Would it have been more simple if a slave was called a slave? Most sensible people probably would think so. It just goes to show how in this particular instance, the framers did not intend to put the word "slave" in the Constitution. They did not want the Constitution to show that a person could own another person. But the language they used actually described just what a slave was held to: labor and service. They wanted to be inclusive. This is a quote taken directly from the *Congressional Globe*, Thirty-sixth Congress, Second Session, page 477, left column:

> Another proposition is that this possession of slave property is a constitutional right and as such ought to be forever recognized by the Federal Government. If the Federal Government shall fail to secure this right, the Southern States should be found united in its defense – in which event Missouri will share the common duties and common danger of the South. This discord prevailing for forty years between the people of the Northern and Southern States, touching the relation of the Federal Government to slavery, affords sufficient reason for all sections of the Union to require a clear and final settlement of all matters in dispute by amendments to the Constitution, so that the slavery question may never again disturb the public peace or impair the national harmony.

The reader must know that when Northerners and Southerners were having disputes about slavery, it was not about freeing Black people. The North did not want slavery to go into the western territories to form new slave States. It was to keep the western territories free to be the home of free White people. It was a political issue (reference: *Congressional Globe*, Thirty-sixth Congress, Second Session, page 477, left column).

Amendments that were proposed to protect slavery included the Crittenden Compromise and the Corwin Amendment (which would have become the Thirteenth Amendment).

Let us take a look at this direct quote:

> The Supreme Court of the United States – the ablest and most impartial tribunal known to the country – uninfluenced by party claim or party feeling, have decided that we [talking about Southerners, especially Southern slave owners] have a right under the Constitu-

tion to go to all the territories of the United States with our slave property, and have it protected (*Congressional Globe*, Thirty-sixth Congress, Second Session, page 569, left column).

I hope this helps to settle what was spoken about earlier when the Northern States and Southern States were having disputes about slavery. The Supreme Court ruled that slavery must be protected in all the territories of the United States and that Southerners had a right to emigrate to them with their slaves. The Kansas-Nebraska Act and the Dred Scott case affirm this; also please remember the words "Federal Laws."

CHAPTER FIVE
Supreme Court Cases That Protected and Supported Slavery

◆ ◆ ◆

Prigg vs. Pennsylvania

This is a quote from the Appendix to the *Congressional Globe* (Thirty-first Congress, Second Session, "The Fugitive Slave Law," messengers Dickinson, Rhett, and Berrien, page 317, Year 1851):

> But I think that all the senator from Georgia read from the message of the Governor of New York was entirely prior to the decision of the case of *Prigg vs. Pennsylvania*. He read from the message of Governor Marcy. If I understood the principles of that decision in the case of *Prigg vs. Pennsylvania*, the Supreme Court goes so far as to say that the whole duty of fulfilling the article of the Constitution in relation to the reclamation of fugitive slaves devolves upon the United States Government, and the United States Government alone.

Even though this decision shows the Supreme Court sanctioning and supporting slavery, Northern States used this an excuse not to return fugitive slaves, violating the U.S. Constitution, Article IV, Section 2, Clause 3. This

Supreme Court decision put the responsibility on the Federal Government to return fugitive slaves to their owners. Northern States repealed their laws to return fugitive slaves. They wanted to leave it up to the U. S. Government to return slaves to their owners.

Cohen vs. Virginia and Lufborough vs. Blake

These cases concern taxes on slaves that would be so high it would force the owners to free them in Washington, D.C. Here is the actual quote:

> An honorable Senator from Vermont (Mr. Prentiss), while delivering his sentiments the other day upon this subject [slavery], expressed the opinion that when legislating for this district, we acted as a local legislature. That Congress possessed the power to levy a tax of such a character upon the slaves of this District [Washington, D.C.] as would, from its amount, force the owners to liberate them in preference to paying the tax. I have a high respect for the intelligence and legal attainments of the Senator from Vermont, but presume he has not investigated this part of his argument with his usual diligence, otherwise he would have found that neither of these questions was yet to be settled. They have been heretofore fully discussed and solemnly decided on by the Supreme Court in the cases of *Cohen vs. Virginia*, and *Lufborough vs. Blake*. The power of Congress to exercise exclusive jurisdiction over this District and other ceded places, is conferred on that body as the Legislature of the United States, and cannot be exercised in any other character.

This shows that Congress could not tax slaves so high that it would force the owners to free them. It would have been an abuse of power.

CHAPTER SIX
The Constitution Protected Property in Slaves

◆ ◆ ◆

The Constitution was adapted to the institution of slavery as it then existed and was in accordance with the public sentiment of the whole country at the time. Accordingly, no man doubted that it RECOGNIZED PROPERTY IN SLAVES and was designed to protect it wherever the national flag was unfurled, on sea or on land (*Congressional Globe*, Senate, Thirty-sixth Congress, Second Session, page 357, middle column).

The second proposition, "That PROPERTY IN SLAVES shall be entitled to the same PROTECTION from the Government of the United States, in all of its departments, everywhere, which the Constitution confers that power upon it to extend to any other property, provided nothing herein contained shall be construed to limit or restrain the right now belonging to every state to prohibit, abolish, or establish and protect SLAVERY within its limits." We demand of the Common Government to use its granted powers to PROTECT OUR PROPERTY as well as yours. This very property is subjected to taxation. It has been taxed by you, and sold by you for taxes. The title to thousands and TENS OF THOU-

SANDS OF SLAVES is derived from the United States. We claim that the Government, while the Constitution recognizes our property for purposes of taxation, shall give it the same protection that it gives yours (*Congressional Globe*, Senate, Thirty-sixth Congress, Second Session, page 268, left column).

"No person held to service or labor in one State under the laws thereof, escaping into another, shall, in consequence of any law or regulation therein, be discharged from such service or labor, but shall be delivered up on claim of the party to whom such service or labor may be due" [reference: Article IV, Section 2, Clause 3 of the United States Constitution]. This language is plain and everybody understood it the same way for the first forty years of our government. In 1793, in Washington's time, an act was passed in the Senate of the United States and nearly so in the House of Representatives. Nobody then had invented pretexts to show that the Constitution did not mean a NEGRO SLAVE. It was plain, it was clear (*Congressional Globe*, Senate, Thirty-sixth Congress, Second Session, page 268, middle column).

Resolved, that the following article be made and is hereby proposed and submitted as an amendment to the Constitution of the United States. "No amendment shall be made to the Constitution which will authorize or give to Congress the power to abolish, or interfere, within any State, with the domestic institutions thereof, including that of persons held to labor or service by the laws of said State" (*Congressional Globe*, Thirty-sixth Congress, Second Session, page 768, left column).

That the possession of SLAVE PROPERTY IS A CONSTITUTIONAL RIGHT, and as such, ought to be ever recognized by the Federal Government. That, if the Federal Government shall fail and refuse to secure this right, the Southern States should be found united in its defense – in which event Missouri will share the common duties and common danger of the South. That this discord prevailing for forty years between the people of the Northern and Southern States, touching the relation of the Federal Government to slavery, afford sufficient reason for all sections of the Union to require a clear and final settlement of all matters in dispute, by amendment to the Constitution, so that the slavery question may never again disturb the public peace or impair the National harmony (*Congressional Globe*, Thirty-sixth Congress, Second Session, page 477, left column).

The Supreme Court of the United States – the ablest and most impartial tribunal known to the country – uninfluenced by party clamor and party feeling, have decided that we have the right under the Constitution, to go to all the territories of the United States with our SLAVE PROPERTY, and have it PROTECTED (*Congressional Globe*, Thirty-sixth Congress, Second Session, Page 569, left column).

"That SLAVES ARE PROPERTY, and regarded as such by the Constitution, has been determined by the highest authority, by every department of our Government and the great mass of the prominent Statesmen of our Country." The Supreme Court of the United States has decided that the Constitution makes NO DISTINCTION BETWEEN SLAVES AND OTHER PROPERTY and pledges the Government to PROTECT IT. This settled no new principle. The same doctrine was held by the Continental Congress under the Articles of Confederation, and by the administrator of Mr. Madison and the United States Senate, under the Constitution, and in both instances by the wisest and purest men that the world has ever produced: men who pledged their lives, their property, and sacred honor to the maintenance of the rights of the country (*Congressional Globe*, Thirty-sixth Congress, Second Session, Thursday, January 10, 1861, middle column).

If according to the American system polity, SLAVES ARE RECOGNIZED AS PROPERTY, it comes within the constitutional guarantee, and the FEDERAL GOVERNMENT IS BOUND TO PROTECT IT THE SAME AS OTHER PROPERTY, wherever it has jurisdiction. Then, whether slaves are constitutionally recognized as property, is a question first to be settled by everyone who would be earnest in his politics, or faithful in the discharge of his duty as a citizen. If the South have a constitutional right to slave property, the same as all other property, should be protected within the scope of the jurisdiction of the Federal Government, and the North will not submit to such constitutional guarantee, in justice and fair dealings, the South ought not to be held to submit to the bonds of union. When it is determined that the North will not live by the Constitution, can it be claimed in fairness that the South shall? If not, then it becomes the North to grant everything that the Constitution secures, or submit to a dissolution of the Union, and disintegration of the whole national system of government (*Congressional Globe*, Thirty-sixth Congress, Second Session, Thursday, January 10, 1861).

The Crittenden Adjustment – Crittenden Compromise. Mr. English offered the following resolution and moved the previous question on its adoption: Resolved, that the present alarming condition of the country imperatively demands that Congress should take immediate steps to preserve the peace and maintain the Union, by removing as far as possible, all causes of irritation and division, and to that end patriotism should prompt a cheerful surrender of all partisan prejudices and minor differences of opinion; and this House, believing the plan of adjustment proposed by Hon. John J. Crittenden, in the Senate, December 16, 1860, would be an equitable and honorable compromise, involving no sacrifice to any party or section that should not promptly be made for the sake of the inestimable blessing of peace and united country, hereby instruct the Committee of Thirty-Three heretofore appointed by the House to report, without delay, the necessary measures to carry that plan into practical effect (*Congressional Globe*, House of Representatives, Thirty-sixth Congress, Second Session, page 498, middle column).

Our property, that is, the property of the South, which, like any other article of personal property, may be transferred from one State or territory to another, consists mostly in SLAVES. It is a PROPERTY RECOGNIZED BY THE CONSTITUTION; for that instrument expressly provides for its capture and rendition when it has escaped from one State to another (*Congressional Globe*, Thirty-third Congress, First Session, page 718).

That vote seemed to be connected with and predicated upon the great fact that the Supreme Court of the United States had decided this question, that they had declared the Missouri Compromise – in other words, the law excluding slavery north of 30° 30' – unconstitutional and void; and according to our forms of Government, it was stricken from the Statute Book by the decision of the Court. They thereby said to the country, the Supreme Arbitrator of the land, so made by the Constitution of the United States, had decided that the people have a right, without regard to the character or description of their property, to carry it into all the territories of the United States, and that under the Constitution of the United States it is protected there. It was said, the Court having decided that they had a right to go there with this institution of SLAVERY and the Constitution finding it there, it was RECOGNIZED AND PROTECTED BY THE CONSTITUTION OF THE UNITED STATES (*Congressional Globe*, Thirty-sixth Congress,

Second Session, page 767).

The Constitution of the United States recognizes SLAVES AS PROPERTY, and pledges the Federal Government to protect it. Congress cannot exercise any more authority over property of that description, than it may constitutionally exercise over property of any other kind.

The territories of the United States are opened to all the people of the United States, with all their property of every kind that is recognized as property by the Constitution of the United States! That the Constitution of the United States recognizes SLAVES AS PROPERTY; that a citizen has a right to go into any territory with his property; that when he enters it with a SLAVE, the Constitution of the United States goes with him and PROTECTS HIM IN THE ENJOYMENT OF THE PROPERTY (*Congressional Globe*, House of Representatives, Thirty-sixth Congress, First Session, page 459, middle column).

The Supreme Court of the United States makes this annunciation. After they had gone on and asserted that the property of a citizen was entitled to protection in any territory of the United States by the Constitution of the United States; that Constitution protected private property; that SLAVES WERE PROPERTY; that the Constitution went with this property into the territories and when a citizen went into a territory with his slave; that the Constitution PROTECTED and DEFENDED IT.

That the only power, which Congress possesses over slavery in the territories, is the power coupled with the duty of guarding and protecting the owner in his rights. This is plainly the decision of the Supreme Court (*Congressional Globe,* House of Representative, Thirty-sixth Congress, First Session, left column, near end, page 459).

The recent legislation of Congress respecting domestic slavery, derived as it has been, from the original and pure fountain of legitimate political power, the will of the majority promises were long to allay the dangerous excitement (*Congressional Globe,* Thirty-sixth Congress, First Session, page 469. left column, near end).

What they claim is that when slavery is established in a territory, if the Territorial Legislature shall fail or refuse, from any cause to pass laws for its security and protection or shall pass laws unfriendly to it thereby, in either case, making an invidious discrimination between SLAVES AND OTHER PROPERTY, it shall be the duty of Congress to provide laws for its PROTECTION – first in case of non-action by the Territorial Legislature directly on application of the slave holder, setting forth the fact; second, in case of unfriendly legislation, directly on such legislation being decided unconstitutional by the Supreme Court of the United States. It may be that such congressional legislation will never be required. But the right to it must not be yielded that its exercise may be demanded whenever the necessity shall. This is simply sustaining the decision of the Supreme Court of the United States by Congressional Legislation. In a word, it is harmonizing the judicial and legislative departments of the Government in support of Constitutional right, which the South cannot surrender and ought not to permit to be sacrificed. When the necessity shall arise to PROTECT SLAVES OR OTHER PROPERTY in the territories, or where the Federal Government had jurisdiction, every department of the Government, legislative, executive and judicial, must be brought to bear to give the protection *(Congressional Globe,* Thirty-sixth Congress, First Session, January 18, 1861, page 510, middle column.)

President Abraham Lincoln says that he prefers

a National convention as the most appropriate mode, but he has no insuperable objections to the other mode, and he will not oppose, but gives us to understand he will favor, the ratification by the States of the amendment already proposed prohibiting any future amendment whereby Congress may be authorized to interfere with slavery in the United States *(Congressional Globe,* Senate Thirty-seventh Congress, Fourth Session, page 1437, right column).

The Senator refers to one amendment: that which was adopted by Congress, with reference to not interfering with slavery in the States. That Mr. Lincoln expresses his willingness to agree to; but will that be satisfactory to the South? (*Congressional Globe*, Thirty-seventh Congress, Fourth Session, page 1438, right column).

If the people, when they came to amend the Constitution, shall determine dial Congress shall have no power upon the subject of slavery anywhere, except to surrender fugitive slaves [to owners] and to prohibit the African slave trade, Mr. Lincoln will not oppose it. If the people shall say that it shall be the duty of Congress to protect slavery everywhere in the territories, Mr. Lincoln is not to oppose that. If, on the contrary, the people shall say that they are in favor the Crittenden Proposition – dividing the territory by a geographical line, on the principle of an equitable partition – Mr. Lincoln says he will not oppose that. He is ill favor of such amendments as will settle the question forever, by and express provision of the Constitution, and he leaves the people and their representatives to devise what those amendments shall be and he will accept them cheerfully, and not draw any obstructions in the way their adoption (*Congressional Globe,* Senate, Thirty-seventh Congress, Fourth Session, page 1438, left column).

He says that Mr. Lincoln is willing, if the people amend the Constitution, to acquiesce in it; that if they think proper to make an amendment recognizing the Crittenden Proposition, Mr. Lincoln will acquiesce in it (page 1438, bottom of middle, top of right column, March 6, 1861).

Sir, I have examined with some care the various propositions submitted to the House for the purpose of quieting the present troubles. The compromises proposed by the chairman of the committee of thirty-three (Mr. Corwin) are as follows:

An amendment to the Constitution, whereby any power to interfere with slavery in the States is forever denied to Congress, until every State in the Union, by its individual State action, shall consent.

An act for the admission of New Mexico as a slave State, without further action of Congress.

An amendment of fugitive slave law, so that it shall be more efficient for the arrest of fugitive slaves.

An amendment of the act for the rendition of fugitives from justice, so as to give the federal courts exclusive jurisdiction, and make the indictment *prima facie* evidence against the accused.

So far as the first proposition is concerned, there is no necessity whatever for its passage. The Constitution protects slavery in the States and forbids any interference by Congress. The platform of the Republican Party, adopted at Chicago, expressly recognizes this doctrine in the following resolve:

"...That the maintenance inviolate of the rights of the States, and especially the right of each State to order and control its own domestic institutions, according to its own judgment exclusively, is essential to that balance of power to which the perfection and endurance of our political fabric depends; and we denounce the lawless invasion by armed force, of the soil of any State or territory, no matter under what pretext, as among the gravest of crimes" [Also look at the Crittenden Compromise].

Mr. Speaker, these amendments make slavery a national institution, by a constitutional recognition of the right of property in man and pledges the Federal Government to its support (*Congressional Globe,* House of Representatives, Thirty-sixth Congress, Second Session, page 980, left and middle column, February 1861).

An explanatory amendment to the Constitution on the subject of slavery. The explanatory amendment might be confined to the final settlement of the true construction of the Constitution on three special parts. 1.An express recognition of the right of PROPERTY IN SLAVES in the States where it now exists or may hereafter exist. 2. The duty of protecting this right in all the common territories throughout their territorial existence, and until they shall be admitted as States into the Union, with or without slavery, as their constitution may prescribe. 3. A like recognition of the right of the master to have his slave, who has escaped from one State to another, restored and "delivered up" to him, and the validity of the fugitive slave law enacted for this purpose, together with a declaration that all State laws impairing or defeating this right are violations of the Constitution, and are consequently null and void. It may be objected that this construction of the Constitution has already been settled by the Supreme Court of the United States. What more ought to be required (*Congressional Globe,* Thirty-sixth Congress, Second Session, page 4, left column, December 1860).

We are presented now with this naked proposition – that Congress shall not interfere with slavery in the States. And that is to quiet all apprehension in the South! Well, sir if we come to vote upon it, I shall vote for it (*Congressional Globe,* Thirty-sixth Congress, Second Session, page 1388, left column.)

I have heard them point to the fact that the North was growing so rapidly that in a very few years the Northern States would have three-fourths and hence might amend the Constitution, and would amend it, so as to abolish slavery in the States. I supposed that those who used it were sincere in it; they had told their people so and made them believe it, and produced this state of insecurity in the mind of Southern people, that produced the necessity of giving this guarantee, that come what may, in all future time, no amendment shall ever be made which will authorize Congress to interfere with the question of slavery in the States (*Congressional Globe,* Thirty-sixth Congress, Second Session, page 1388, left column).

Resolved, that the Constitution of the United States recognizes property in slaves; that Congress has passed laws to aid slaveholders in recapturing their slaves whenever they escaped and make their way into the free States; that the Supreme Court had decided that Negroes were not included, either in the Declaration of Independence or Constitution of the United States, EX-CEPT AS SLAVES, and that they cannot become citizens; and we the members of this House, hereby sustain and will support this construction of the Constitution, these laws, and said decision of the Supreme Court (*Congressional Globe,* House of Representatives, Thirty-sixth Congress, Second Session, page 123, left column, Year 1860).

We are to go to the Southern States, I am to go to my State of Virginia, and say, "you demanded a security for your rights in the common territories, and you have been answered by giving you a plank of the Chicago Platform, declaring that it was not the purpose of

Congress to interfere with slavery in the States. Honorable Senators have told us – the Senator from Illinois has, very frequently – that if this is made a part of the Constitution, it will be irreparable, except by the consent of all the States. By what authority does the Senator say so? Mr. Douglas: because there will be a clause then in the Constitution declaring that no future amendment shall ever authorize Congress to interfere with the question of slavery in the States. That being a part of the Constitution, it will be just as sacred as the clause now in the Constitution, declaring that no future amendment shall ever deprive any State of its two Senators in Congress (*Congressional Globe,* Thirty-sixth Congress, Second Session, page 1387, right column, Year 1861).

But since experience has proved to you that you cannot administer the Government and preserve the Union on your policy of congressional interference, and since you have adopted the doctrine of NON-INTERVENTION as to all territories we now possess, why not just embody that principle in the Constitution, denying the power of Congress over the subject of slavery everywhere in the future? Do this and we shall have peace and harmony in the country. At all events, Sir I am in favor of such amendments to the Constitution as will take that question out of Congress, and restore peace to the country. That may be done by NON-INTERVENTION – by popular sovereignty, as it is called or by the CRITTENDEN AMENDMENT (Compromise) (*Congressional Globe,* Thirty-sixth Congress, Second Session, page 1461, left column, Year 1861).

I begin thus: If the gentlemen means that, in violation of the Constitution of the United States, we of the North or West, by any bill, resolution, or act, do in anywise interfere with the state and condition of slavery where it exists within the States of the Union, or any of them, by virtue of local law, by which alone it can be created. We deny it. We have offered no such interference: We claim no such power. Sir, as I remember the history, as early as 1790, a committee of the House of Representatives composed, with one exception, of NORTHERN MEN – reported to that Congress a resolution, which you will read in the great speech of Mr. Webster upon this point, declaring that we have no right or power to interfere with slavery in the States. That resolution was adopted by a Northern Congress – a body near two-thirds of whom were Northern men: and I say that from that day to this, according my recollection, and in my best judgment, and on my conscience, I do not know, nor do I believe, that Congress has attempted seriously to doubt practically that doctrine, or in any wise to interfere with the condition of slavery in the States.... (*Congressional Globe,* Thirty-sixth Congress, Second Session, page 239, middle column, near end).

No party in the North entertains any purpose of a crusade against slavery in the slave States: no part whatever, in any of the FREE STATES, entertains any such proposal at all. Nobody pretends that Congress has any such power; and therefore, the Senate from Virginia very properly replies it adds nothing: it takes away nothing. When you have done it you have done nothing: you have only said that Congress shall have no power to do what everybody admits Congress had no power to do (Middle Column, page 1392).

It is said here that the Southern States have an apprehension of insecurity, for the institution of slavery in the States. Is that apprehension well founded? Senators upon the other side of the chamber agree that NO PARTY IN THE NORTH has at any time, does now, or threatens hereafter, to establish a policy or claims the right to interfere with slavery in the States at all (*Congressional Globe,* Thirty-sixth Congress, Second Session, page 1392, Bottom of left column).

A. Mr. Lincoln belongs to that wing of the Republican party which asserts this qualified right of property in Persons (slaves), and holds that it is the duty of the Federal Government in all its departments, to yield protection to SLAVE PROPERTY in accordance with that provision of the Constitution which provides for the surrender of fugitive slaves. Hence I do assert that it is not dealing fairly with this subject to say that the Republicans deny that there is any such thing as a Right of Property in a slave. It is unfair to say that the Republican Administration deny that the Federal Government shall protect slave property in any case, for the President has told you in the inaugural that he will protect it [-SLAVE PROPERTY] in the cases provided for in the Constitution.

B. I had hoped, too, that when he referred to these divisions in the Republican Party he would cited that fact that Mr. Lincoln, the President of the United States, was among those who held the doctrine that there is such a thing as a RIGHT OF PROPERTY IN A SLAVE, and hence that the Southern States had a right to demand an efficient fugitive slave law for the return of their slaves. Mr. Lincoln has proclaimed these opinions. He has never taken them back. He hold, therefore, that there is such a legal right of property in a slave as enables the master to reclaim him, and makes it the duty of the Government to protect that right. Then there is a case in which Mr. Lincoln himself recognizes the right and duty of the Federal protection of slave property. He acknowledges the right of Federal protection, the duty of Congress to pass a law affording the Federal protection, the duty of the officers to execute the law and he has proclaimed in the inaugural [address] his purpose to carry out the law, and furnish that Federal protection according to laws of the land.

C. Hence we have no excuse, no pretext for dissolving the Union, so far as the territorial question is concerned. Then, what more should he tell them? He should tell them that, having got their rights in the territories, he was gratified to be able to say also, that, not withstanding the party pressure, the last Congress had by a vote of two thirds, proposed an amendment to the Constitution prohibiting any future amendment by which Congress could ever interfere with slavery in the States. "Thus," he could say, "we have two assurances: one that our rights shall never be violated in the territories, and another that they shall never be violated in the States of the Union" (*Congressional Globe,* Thirty-sixth Congress, Second Session, page 1509, left and middle columns).

CHAPTER SEVEN
Washington D.C. is the
Real Slave Capital

◆ ◆ ◆

Washington, D.C. was established as the capital of the United States by the Residency Act of 1793 on land that was donated by two slave-holding States: Maryland and Virginia. After Washington, D.C. was established, the U.S. Congress passed laws to support, protect, and establish slavery there (also the coastwise slave trade). This to me makes Washington D.C. our slaveholding capital under the American flag with the approval and acceptance of our Congress. George Washington was our President during this time. His name is also signed to a Fugitive Slave Law along with another U.S. President, Milliard Fillmore. If this is not the official U.S. endorsement of slavery – its protection and support – I do not know what is. Here is the reference: Appendix to the *Congressional Globe*, Thirty-second Congress, First Session: "The Fugitive Slave Law," Mr. Badger, Senate, page 1116).

Washington D.C. also had slave pens to keep slaves until they could be sold or shipped somewhere else. Here is the direct quote:

Now sir, if the gentleman means to say that he has no personal knowledge of "slave pens" and of the slave traffic in this District [Washington, D. C.], that is one thing; but if he means to deny or call in question the existence of the traffic itself, or the dens where its concentrated iniquities make up the daily employment of men, that is quite another thing. Sir, from the Western Front of this capital, from the piazza that opens out from your Congressional Library, as you cast your eye along the horizon and over the conspicuous objects of the landscape – the President's Mansion – you cannot fail to see the horrid and black receptacles where HUMAN BEINGS ARE PENNED LIKE CATTLE – as strictly and literally so as oxen and swine are kept and sold at the Smithfield Shambles in London, or at the cattle fair in Brighton. In a communication made during the last session, by the mayor of this city to an honorable member of this house, he acknowledges the EXISTENCE OF SLAVE PENS HERE (*Congressional Globe*, appendix, Thirtieth Congress, second session, February 23, 1849, page 318).

More Direct Quotes

As citizens of the free States [Northern States], we ask especially that this District may be purified with a thorough lustration, so that the capital of the nation, which should reflect the national honor, shall cease to be trodden by a slave, and the national flag no longer protect slavery and the slave trade under its folds. We ask to be released from the infamy of the TRAFFIC IN MEN, WOMEN, AND CHILDREN, which is often heralded through the city papers to take place almost under the shadow of the U. S. Capitol. Let this foul blot be wiped off from our national escutcheon (Appendix to the *Congressional Globe*, Thirty-sixth Congress, second session, Execution of United States Law, Debate, Senate, page 230).

They should distinctly understand, that while the people of the free States are involved in the support of SLAVERY IN THIS DISTRICT, or of the coastwise slave trade; while Congress lends its powers and influence to rob a portion of the people of their inalienable rights – Northern philanthropy and Northern patriotism will make their voices heard in this hall nor will they silenced until this District is rendered free, until the nation's flag shall cease to float over cargoes of slaves, and the territories of the United States shall be exempt from the curse of oppression. We wish to deceive no one. We desire all to understand our position. We base our efforts distinctly upon the letter and the spirit of the Constitution. Separation of this government and the people of the free States from all participation in the support of slavery, constitute our object nor shall we relax our exertions while a slave shall be held as such under the Laws of Congress (Appendix to the *Congressional Globe*, Thirtieth Congress, Second Session, Relation of the Federal Government to Slavery, Mr. Giddings, House of Representatives, page 128).

In the case of *Mahoney vs. Ashton*, where a Negro woman was carried by her owners as a slave from the island of Barbados to England, and afterwards brought to Maryland, it was held, after full and elaborate argument, that however the laws of Great Britain operate upon persons there claimed as slaves, might interfere to prevent acts of ownership, yet upon bringing the slave into Maryland the relation of master and slave continued: that the condition of slaves does not depend exclusively either on the civil or the feudal law. Our act of Congress regulating and protecting the conveying Negro slaves coastwise, necessarily repudiates the idea of slavery being solely existent and valid in the place of its domicile. As property, like every other variety, it is subject to the general legislation of Congress, to guard, protect, and facilitate its safe and easy removal from one place to another; and THE GOVERNMENT OF THE UNITED STATES IS BOUND TO PROTECT IT, unless it be taken to a foreign country for permanency, where its continuance is prohibited by local law (Appendix to the *Congressional Globe*, Thirty-fourth Congress, First Session, "The Slavery Question," Mr. Stewart, House of Representatives, page 985, Year 1856).

American liberty is understood to mean the liberty to oppress, THE LIBERTY TO ENSLAVE, the liberty to imbrute our fellow men; and one foreign writer has even suggested that our national emblem should be made truly emblematic of our real character, by picturing the eagle with liberty on his wings and with a Negro chained and writhing in talons, and his heart's blood dripping from his beak (Appendix to the *Congressional Globe*, Thirty-third Congress, Second Session, Senate, page 230, left column).

Justice, humanity, liberty, patriotism, all implore us to banish SLAVERY FROM THE NATIONAL GLOBE and everywhere to absolve the Federal Government from its guilty complicity with slavery (Appendix to the Congressional Globe, Thirty-third Congress, Second Session, Senate, page 230, middle column).

The Federal Government and Slavery

By another law in force here, by the Enactment and Authority of the United States, ANY COLORED PERSON, free or bond, coming into the National District is liable to be seized and imprisoned as a fugitive from slavery; and if unable in that helpless and forlorn situation, to pay all fees and rewards given by law for apprehending runaways, is LIABLE TO BE SOLD INTO SLAVERY FOR LIFE to the highest bidder; and to crown the atrocity, the price of blood – the "money or tobacco," as the law reads – shall go into the pockets of the marshal himself – the judge in the case – as imprisonment fees, except what may be needed to pay for the arrest of the victim – thus holding out a bribe to the marshal to adjudge him to slavery. Under this law several persons, according to the reports of the marshals, not having been claimed as slaves, and therefore presumed to be free, have been sold into slavery for life. Thus the Government sells its own citizens into slavery, as cannibals sometimes eat their own children....

By the authority of the United States, there appeared in this city a few days since, under the meridian sun, a human shape on horseback, dragging a woman by a rope around her body through its muddy streets. With unblushing face, and head erect, gloating over his victim with a spider-like exultation, this gallant son of "the chivalry," ascended the hill on which we are assemble, with his human prey, and passed by under the very shadow of the Capitol over which at that moment your national flag was proudly floating as the ensign of freedom. Oh, "that model Republic!" – the great slave monger, the great slave market, the great slavery propaganda of the nineteenth century AROUND WHOSE CAPITAL MEN ARE BOUGHT AND SOLD LIKE OXEN, AND WOMEN ARE HUNTED AND LED AS SAVAGES HUNT AND LEAD BUFFALOES BY THE LASSO! (Appendix to the *Congressional Globe*, Thirty-third Congress, Second Session, Senate, page 228, middle column).

I will tell you, Mr. President, just what our position is in Massachusetts. We stand upon the impregnable basis of the Constitution of the United States. We do not propose to encroach upon the rights of our Southern brethren, but we claim that under the express authority of the Constitution of the United States, we have ample power to abolish slavery in the District of Columbia. We of Massachusetts, and of the free States, are responsible for THE EXISTENCE OF HUMAN SLAVERY HERE IN THE NATIONAL CAPITAL. Slavery exists here by the authority or rather by the permission of Congress; and the people of New England, of the central States, and of the West are as responsible for its existence as are the sons of Maryland and Virginia whose ancestors planted it here (Appendix to the *Congressional Globe*, Thirty-third Congress, Second Session, Senate, page 238).

The maintenance of SLAVERY IN THE FEDERAL DISTRICT, by the authority of the United States, exerts a conservative influence over the institution in the States, by clothing it with the countenance and sanction of the nation. THE DISTRICT OF COLUMBIA IS THUS MADE THE CITADEL OF AMERICAN SLAVERY, its munitions of defense, or as the late Mr. Calhoun once said, "THE VERY KEY OF SLAVERY" (Appendix to the *Congressional Globe*, Thirty-third Congress, Second Session, Senate, page 229).

Taxes

He held in his hand an extract from the Act of 1815, imposing direct taxes, which was to be found in the 3rd volume of United States Statutes, page 172. He would read an extract from section 24: "That the annual amount of TAXES so assessed shall constitute a lien upon all the real estate and all the SLAVES of individuals who may be assessed for the same." There was not only a TAX imposed upon SLAVES AS PROPERTY, but it was made to constitute a lien upon each slave for two years from the time the tax law was passed. Well in the 29th section of the act, it was provided, "If the property shall not sell for the amount of the taxes, it shall be lawful to buy it in for the GOVERNMENT OF THE UNITED STATES" (*Congressional Globe*).

The Federal Government has disfranchised the COLORED MEN of the District of Columbia and left them to be plundered of their money under the specious name of TAXES, in the disbursement of which they have no voice, and no direct benefit – thus holding to their lips the same bitter choice of oppression which our revolutionary fathers dashed from theirs with indignant scorn. TAXATION without representation they could not endure – but this Government has inflicted the same intolerable wrong upon the colored man (Appendix to the *Congressional Globe*, Thirty-third Congress, Second Session, Senate, page 230).

Washington, D.C. as a Slave Capital

This is taken directly from the Appendix to the *Congressional Globe*, Thirtieth Congress, Second Session, House of Representatives:

They should distinctly understand, that while the people of the free States are involved in the SUPPORT OF SLAVERY IN THIS DISTRICT, or of the coastwise slave trade; while Congress lends its powers and influence to rob a portion of the people of their inalienable rights – Northern philanthropy and Northern patriotism will make their voices heard in this hall. Nor will they be silenced until this District is rendered free, until the national flag shall cease to float over cargoes of slaves, and the territories of the United States shall be exempt from the curse of oppression. We wish to deceive no one. We desire all to understand our position. We base our efforts distinctly upon the letter and the spirit of the Constitution. Separation of the Federal Government and the people of the free States from all participation in the support of slavery constitute our object. Nor shall we relax our exertions while a slave shall be held as such under the laws of Congress (Appenpendix to the *Congressional Globe*, Thirtieth Congress, Second Session, House of Representatives, p. 128).

The slave laws of the District, no one will deny, were enacted by the Congress of the United States, approved by the President of the United States, and they are enforced by the authority of the United States, in a District over which Congress has "exclusive" jurisdiction in all cases whatsoever by the CONSTITUTION OF THE UNITED STATES."

Clearly then Congress – having enacted laws by which MEN ARE HELD IN SLAVERY IN THIS DISTRICT – can hasten to their relief, knock off their chains, and restore to them their plundered rights, their long-lost manhood.

But Mr. President, I deem it necessary to pursue the argument further on this point, since the POWER OF CONGRESS OVER SLAVERY IN THE DISTRICT has been admitted by the highest authorities in the country and in 1850 conceded by Congress itself, by the passing of a law prohibiting the importation of slaves into the District for sale. If Congress can abolish the slave market here, can it not strike another blow at the root of the complicated wrong, and abolish slavery itself? If it can forbid traffic in men, can it not forbid the enslavement of men – by repealing laws of its own enacting which make men slaves? (Appendix to the *Congressional Globe*, Thirty-third Congress, Second Session, Senate, 1855, page 229, right column; reference: footnote one, Appendix to *Congressional Globe*, Thirtieth Congress, Second Session, House of Representatives, page 128).

CHAPTER EIGHT
The U.S. Congress Passed Laws to Protect and Support Slavery

◆ ◆ ◆

The U.S. Congress, our law-making body for the United States, at one time passed laws to protect and support slavery, also to establish the coastwise slave trade. This may be embarrassing or shocking to some people to learn, but it is the truth. I hope that people who have any doubts would carefully study this section, even read it two or three times, because the truth can sometimes be too difficult to digest or accept, but it can be digested. This kind of stuff is not regularly written about in our politically-correct history books. People who write our history books and other books tell lies or half-truths in them. They even omit true facts about history. They write history books and other books with a left wing slant to them. Take for instance the lie that has been told in our history books and encyclopedia books today, that slavery was the cause of the Civil War. That is an ugly lie. Read the Crittenden Resolution, passed in July 1861. It affirms that the Civil War was being fought to preserve the Union and not to end slavery. It was passed by the U.S. Congress.

Take for instance another example: There were two U.S. major generals who freed some slaves in their military districts. Guess what Abraham Lincoln did? He fired one – Major General John C. Fremont – and sent the slaves back to their owners. The other major general, David Hunter, obeyed Lincoln and changed his emancipation order. Lincoln sent those slaves back to their owners also. If slavery was the cause of the Civil War, as some lying historians say, why would Abraham Lincoln, the U.S. President, do this? One reason why he revoked those General Emancipation Orders was to keep border slave-holding States like Kentucky and Missouri in the Union. I hope you, the reader, get some idea of how far history is or can be slanted.

Looking at some of the quotes in this section may be disturbing, but they are real. Here is one that shows two U.S. Presidents who used their office to support and sustain slavery. It is also true that Mr. Van Buren, while President, followed the example of General (later President) Andrew Jackson in lending the influence of his office to sustain the coastwise slave trade. In this he complied with a vowed opinion of the U.S. Senate. That august body adopted resolutions as late as 1840 unanimously declaring it to be the duty of the Government to protect those who were engaged in that detestable traffic – the slave trade (reference: Appendix to the *Congressional Globe*, Thirtieth Congress, second session, Relation of the Federal Government to Slavery, Mr. Giddings, p. 128, right column).

Here is another quote to back this one up:

The stoppage of the coastwise slave trade has also been demanded: but before any petitions for this object has been presented, Congress, by direct legislation, had taken this traffic under its protection, prescribing all the details (reference: Appendix to the *Congressional Globe*, "Union of the Democracy, Resolutions of '98," Mr. Townsend, Thirty-second Congress, first session, House of Representatives, page 346).

Okay, let us check out this quote. It shows President Andrew Jackson again using the office of the Presidency to support and sustain slavery:

> Yet all will agree that if General Jackson had the Constitutional right to exert the influence of this nation to support the slave-trade, it is the duty of the Government to enforce the demands of the slave dealers on board the *Enterprise*, the *Hermosa*, and the *Creole*, even at the expense of our blood and treasure. No school boy would admit that our duty would be limited to a mere demand for reparation; that when a demand is made, our duty to the slave dealers ceases, and the Government is to be absolved from all further notice of their interests (reference: Appendix to the *Congressional Globe*, "Indemnity for Slaves," Mr. Giddings, Twenty-seventh Congress, Third Session, House of Representatives, February 1848, page 195).

Here is another quote that shows that the President of the United States used his office to support slavery. That his devotion to the slave power was openly and boldly avowed might shock some people today:

> Agitation has brought to the scaffold another conspicuous victim. The President of the United States lent his whole influence to the promotion of those compromise measures to which I have alluded. His devotion to the slave power has been openly and boldly avowed. Steadily and basely has he prostituted the influence and power of his office, to the purpose of supporting slavery, oppression, and crime (reference: Appendix to the

Congressional Globe, "Baltimore Platforms, Slavery Question," Mr. Giddings, House of Representatives, Thirty-second Congress, First Session, page 740).

Another part of that same article says this:

All our action under the Constitution should be to protect the life and liberty of every human being within our exclusive jurisdiction. That our legislative powers in this District, on the high seas, and in our territories, should be exerted to secure every human being who bears God's image, in his right to life and liberty, instead of establishing and sustaining oppression, and slavery (reference: same as above).

The next quote also will show that the U.S. Government established and supported slavery in Washington D.C.:

Mr. President, here I might pause; but it may not be amiss to glance at the subsequent policy of a Government which signalized its inauguration by re-establishing slavery in the metropolis of the nation, and expose its profligacy in pandering to the vilest despotism beneath the sun. Although the Constitution of the United States makes no distinction on account of complexion, and admits no right or disqualification, therefore its administrators have taken it upon themselves, in utter violation of its letter and spirit, to proscribe all whiteless persons, and legislate them out of the pale of its protection. Never has a Government been guilty of a more audacious usurpation of power, or a grosser violation of constitutional prerogative. Let us glance at the proscriptive crusade of the Federal Government against a part of the people of this country. Its first act in this direction, as we have seen, was the enactment of the whole slave code, and the reinstitution and perpetuation of slavery in the Federal District.

The part you have just read proves how the U.S. Government supported, sustained, and endorsed slavery. Now here are the direct quotes:

Direct Quotes

There were two fugitive slave laws that were passed by the United States to help slave owners to recapture their fugitive slaves. One was in 1793 and the other in 1850:

The law of 1793 – the first example of national legislation on the subject [slavery] was passed at the demand of the friends of slavery, to enable them to recapture their fugitive slaves with great facility. This law not only gave national aid to a State institution, which is declared to be no concern of ours, but it was an unconstitutional assumption of power on the part of the U.S. Congress, violating the sovereignty of all the free States. By another act of Congress, the Federal Government became responsible for the existence of slavery in this District [Washington, D.C.] more or less ever since; and this, doubtless, to please the friends of slavery. At different periods, North Carolina and Georgia made cessions of territory to the United States, out of which, Kentucky, Tennessee, Alabama, and Mississippi were formed. Congress accepted the cession of the territory with an expressed proviso – a sort of anti-Wilmot proviso – that Congress should never abolish slavery there. Thus giving at the desire of the friends of slavery, a national, though unconstitutional guarantee for its security in those territories. France and Spain ceded Louisiana and Florida to the United States. The treaties [international law] of cession required the United States to secure the blessings of liberty to all the inhabitants; yet Congress was induced to tolerate slavery there, forgetting, perhaps, that the Federal Government was formed for a nobler purpose than the protection of slave property (reference: Appendix to the *Congressional Globe*, Thirty-second Congress, First Session, "Union of the Democracy, Resolution of '98," Mr. Townsend, House of Representatives, March 17, 1852, page 346).

The stoppage of the coastwise slave trade had also been demanded: but before any petitions for this object had been presented, Congress, by direct legislation, had taken this traffic under its protection and regulation, prescribing all the details (same reference as above).

The slave States early finding themselves unable to hold their bondmen [slaves] in subjection [slavery], called on the Federal Government to assist them in recovering their fugitives [slaves] from their neighbors, the Indians. Without discussion, or so far as we know, without objection, the Executive power then, as usual in slave holding hands, effected a treaty providing for the return of fugitive slaves to their masters (reference: Appendix to the *Congressional Globe*, "The Compromise Measures, Fugitive Slave Law," Mr. Giddings, Thirty-second Congress, First Session, House of Representatives, March 16, 1852, page 772).

But Congress in 1793 passed a law, to which reference was made yesterday, by which Congress declares that the master shall be entitled to seize or arrest his fugitive slave whenever he shall escape from him into another State of the Union (Appendix to the Congressional Globe, Thirty-first Congress, First Session, "The Fugitive Slave Bill," Mr. Pratt, Senate, Year 1850, page 1273).

Mr. President, I shudder when I think of these expressions; because if there be any truth in them, they are just as applicable to George Washington as they are to Millard Fillmore. George Washington's name is signed to a fugitive slave law, liable to every objection applicable to this one signed by Millard Fillmore, and he is just as liable to these imputations. If Millard Fillmore is to be consigned to the lowest depths of infamy because he signed the Fugitive Slave law, then if there is any justice or equality in the judgment of mankind, George Washington should receive the same fate from posterity and us....

We demand the abolition of the domestic slave trade, so far as it can be constitutionally reached: but particularly on the high seas under the national flag. And generally we demand from the Federal Government, the exercise of all its constitutional power to relieve itself from the responsibility for slavery. And yet one thing further must be done. The slave power must be overturned, so that the Federal Government may be openly, actively, and perpetually on the side of freedom (reference: Appendix to the *Congressional Globe*, Thirty-second Congress, First Session, "The Fugitive Slave Law," Mr. Badger, Senate, page 116).

The Constitution of the United States, in the clauses securing the right of reclamation of fugitive slaves, forbidding their foreign importation after the year 1808, and apportioning representatives and direct taxes, recognize the existence of such an institution [slavery]. The quibbles about the words "held to service" not including the idea, and referring to slavery as then and now existing in many of the States, is mere chicanery. The Supreme Court of the United States, in passing upon these clauses, recognizes slaves as property (Appendix to the *Congressional Globe*, Thirtieth Congress, Second Session, "The Tariff and Slavery Questions," Mr. J. B. Thompson, 1849, page 97).

CHAPTER NINE
International Law (Treaties)

◆   ◆   ◆

Before we get to how slaves were protected by treaties of the United States with other countries, let us read some about treaties first, to really see how powerful they are, especially when they are really enforced. Treaties are an agreement (or laws) among two or more nations. They are also part of international law. International law is what civilized nations live under in peacetime or in wartime. Let us see how treaties are established according to the Constitution.

Article 6 states: "This Constitution, and the laws of the United States which shall be made pursuant thereof, and all treaties made or which shall be made under the authority of the United States, shall be the supreme law of the land, and the judges in every State shall be bound thereby, anything in the Constitution or laws of any State to the contrary notwithstanding." The Constitution of the United States confers absolutely on the Government the power of making war and of making treaties. Consequently, that Government possesses the power of acquiring territory, either by conquest or by treaty (*The American Insurance Company v. 356 Bales of Cotton*). The obligation of a treaty, the supreme law of the land, must be admitted. The execution of the contract between the two nations or more is to be demanded from the executive of each nation, but where a treaty affects the right of parties litigating in court, the treaty as much binds those rights and is as much regarded by the Supreme Court as an act of Congress (*United States v. The Schooner Peggy*). The termination of a treaty, by war, does not divest rights of property already vested under it (*Society for the Propagation of the Gospel vs. The Town of New Haven*). One example was the Treaty of Ghent, in which Great Britain had to pay the United States for the loss of slaves during the War of 1812. You will read more about that later. Nor do treaties, in general, become extinguished, *ipso facto*, by war between the two governments. Those stipulating for a permanent arrangement of territorial and other national rights are at peacetime unless they are waived by the parties or new and repugnant stipulations are made. Where a treaty is the law of the land, and as such affects the rights or parties litigating in court, that treaty as much binds those rights and is as much to be regarded by the court as an act of Congress. To condemn vessel, therefore, the restoration of which is directed by the law of the land, though restoration be an executive act, would be a direct infraction of that law and of consequence, improper (*United States vs. The Schooner Peggy*).

A treaty under the Sixth Article, Section 2, of the Constitution, being the supreme law of the land, the treaty of peace of 1783 operated as a repeal of all State laws previously enacted, inconsistent with it provisions (*Ware vs. Hylton*). Whenever a right grows out of or is protected by a treaty, it prevails against all laws or decisions of the courts of the States, and whoever may have the right under the treaty is protected, but if the person's title is not affected by the treaty, if he claims nothing under the treaty, his title cannot be protected. In the United States, a different principle is established. Our Constitution declares a treaty to be the law of the land. It is consequently to be regarded in courts of justice as equivalent to an act of the legislature, whenever it operates of itself, without the aid of any legislative provision. But when the terms of the stipulations import a contract, when either of the parties engages to perform a particular act, the treaty addresses itself to the political, not the judicial department and the legislature must execute the contract before it can become a rule for the court. The stipulations of a treaty are to be understood by its language and apparent intention, manifested in the instrument, with a reference to the contracting parties, the subject matter, and the persons on whom it is to operate (*United States vs. Arredando*).

A treaty of cession is a deed of ceded territory, and the sovereign is the grantor; the act is his, as far as it relates to the cession; the treaty is his fact and deed, and all courts must so consider it and deeds are construed in equity by the rules of law. Where a treaty is executed in two languages, each language of the respective contracting parties, both parts of the treaty are originals, and both are intended to convey the same meaning. Where a treaty has been ratified according to the provisions of the Constitution, it becomes the law of the land and it is perfectly immaterial, whether or not the person who signed it did or did not transcend their instructions *(Hamilton vs. Eaton)*.

A treaty does not necessarily annul prior statutes, if there is no interference with them. The stipulation in a treaty between the United States and a foreign power is paramount to the provisions to the Constitution of a particular State (*Lessee of Harry Gordon vs. Kerr*). A treaty between the United States and one belligerent, does not affect a question of prize, as between two belligerents, where the prize [captured from the belligerent making the treaty] is brought by the other belligerent into the ports of the United States, nor is it important that the capturing vessel was commanded by an American citizen. The treaty can bind only the parties to it, and whatever operation it may have on the American citizen, individually, it cannot affect the general question of the validity of prizes made between belligerents.

A judgment of a State court, where jurisdiction was acquired by the common law, but by a statute of a State, which, before the rendition of the judgment, had been virtually repealed and not void (*Livingston vs. Van Ingen*). In 1780, the ancestor of the lessors of the plaintiff was indicted, he being a British subject, in the supreme court of New York, under the act titled "An Act for the Forfeiture and Sale of the Property of this State" and in October 1783, a judgment of forfeiture against his estates was rendered. The adoption of a treaty with the stipulations of which is the provisions of a State law are inconsistent and is equivalent to the repeal of such law (*Lessee of Hylton vs. Brown*).

Now let us talk about the Treaty of Ghent protecting slaves along with other property. This quote is taken directly from the Twentieth Congress, First Session, House of Representatives, "Claims of Indemnity for Slaves and Other Property Under the First Article of the Treaty of Ghent, March 10, 1828," page 474:

> To the honorable, the House of Representatives: A memorial in behalf of the Virginia and Maryland claimants under the First Article of the Treaty of Ghent. The claim for slaves and other private property grew out of the First Article of the Treaty of Ghent. The Government of the United States and Great Britain, widely differing as to the construction of the said article, submit-

ted the whole subject to the decision and award of the Emperor of Russia. Upon the rendition of his award, his further mediation was invoked to have prepared a convention at St. Petersburg, to carry into effect the object of his award, as expounding the First Article of the Treaty of Ghent. A mixed commission was constituted soon after, which met in the city of Washington, D.C. After continuing from 1824 until 1826, it was well ascertained that the British and American Commissioners would never agree as to the true construction of the said convention. They submitted the points of difference and their argument to their respective Governments, and Mr. Gallatin, the minister of the United States, concluded with the British Government, the convention of London, in November 1826, which was duly ratified. In the said last convention it was stipulated, in effect, that the British Government was to be wholly released and exonerated from all claims for slaves and other private property, upon the payment of $1,204,960.

This material was taken directly from the U.S. Government Documents and Debates paperwork.

The next quote is taken from the *Congressional Globe*, Thirty-sixth Congress, Second Session, page 357, middle column: "Thus we see, that the law making and the treaty-making powers of our Government – Congress and the Executive – have each considered slaves as property, and have repeatedly and uniformly treated them as such." This was done in Jay's Treaty. It was done in the Treaty of Ghent, and the Treaty for the Acquisition of Louisiana which recognizes and protects the right of property in slaves.

CHAPTER TEN
War Crimes and War Criminals

◆　◆　◆

War crimes are crimes that are committed against people and property during war. War criminals are the people who commit those crimes. Under international law (laws of war, laws of nations), non-combatants are not supposed to be harmed and unnecessary destruction of property (including personal property) is a crime. International law is what nations operate under during peace time and during war. Not all nations accept all rules of international law. International law is also hard to enforce, especially if nations do not want to go before an arbitration court to settle their differences. Customs and rules for international law were developed over a period of a thousand years. When the Europeans had wars over 200 years, non-combatants were not bothered. Blatant destruction of property was not tolerated. President Abraham Lincoln and the United States Army were the first people to break the civilized rules and codes of modern warfare. The blatant destruction of Southern cities and towns were war crimes. To destroy cities when there were no Confederate soldiers present was a crime. To harm non-combatants and to blatantly destroy Southern peoples' farms and homes also was a war crime. Southern women, White and Black, were raped by Union soldiers. Information like this was left out of our history books, but it can be read about in the following books: *The South Was Right*, by Walter D. and James R. Kennedy, *The Real Lincoln*, by Thomas DiLorenzo, *When in the Course of Human Events*, by Charles Adams, a Northern tax expert. The book *Forced Into Glory: Abraham Lincoln's White Dream* is informative also.

War crimes that were committed against Southern civilians during the Civil War are something that needs to be brought out and dealt with. A true healing process needs to happen. Southerners of all races need to receive some form of reparations and an official apology from the United States Government. Serious war crimes were committed in Maryland and the U.S. Constitution was violated by Abraham Lincoln. Here is the quote taken from the *Congressional Globe*, July 24, 1861, Thirty-seventh Congress, First Session, page 224. A Congressman by the name of Mr. Burnett is speaking. This is one of the extraordinary acts of the Lincoln administration:

> The civil authorities of the State of Maryland have been superseded by order of the President of the United States. A military police establishment has been organized, a violation of the express laws of one of the sovereign States of the United States, either derived from Congress or any other power known to this government. This is done, following another high handed act of aggression upon the rights of private citizens by taking the constituted authorities of the State of Maryland, without authority of law and without probable cause, and incarcerating them in a military fortress of the United States, where they are deprived of their liberty upon a suspension of the Writ of Habeas Corpus by a general acting under the orders of the President of the United States, and that the President himself, violating the Constitution

of the United States, which confers upon Congress alone the right and authority to suspend the Writ of Habeas Corpus. And that does not half paint the picture. Then, when this military police has been put in Baltimore, Maryland, in place of the civil authorities, in violation of the laws of Maryland, and without any authority of Congress – upon a mere order of a military commander, General Banks – when all this has been done, sir, then a bill is introduced into this House asking the Congress of the United States to appropriate $100,000 from the public treasury to pay the men who had been put in this position. My God! Gentlemen, where is this going to end? Gentlemen have again and again repeated that we are in the midst of a revolution. We are, indeed, in the midst of a revolution; not only a revolution against the authorities of the Federal Government in the Southern States, which is horrible enough for any American citizen to contemplate, but a revolution within the government itself, which is known and recognized as the Federal Government. We have set at defiance the Constitution of the country, men in high places, the Chief Magistrate of the United States has violated the plain letter of the U.S. Constitution. He confessed in his message to Congress that he had violated the Constitution, and he justified himself upon the plea of necessity. Yes, sir, resolutions are introduced, one after another, to ratify and endorse all his illegal acts and violations of the Constitution, instead of the representatives of a free people standing up here in their manhood and in their representative capacity, and, high as is the Chief Magistrate of the country, bringing him to the bar of public opinion and there administering to him a just rebuke. I am responsible to my country and to those who sent me here for the faithful discharge of my obligation. I am but a representative. Is his Excellency the President of the United States exempt from censure and rebuke at the hands of the people? What is the condition of the city of Baltimore this day? There are military police there in violation of the laws of the Legislature. There is suspension of the acts of her commissioners, who have been appointed properly, and who so far as I know, or have been able to learn, have been faithfully discharging the duties of their office. Those commissioners, sir, are in prison without authority of law – I may say, in violation of the right of the city, and derogation of the sovereignty of the State of Maryland. Yet while these acts have been done, and are continuing to be done, the chairman of the Committee of Ways and Means comes into this house – when the well regulated police of Baltimore have been superseded by a military police, with an army at the back of it, within the jurisdiction of a sovereign State of the Union – and coolly asks us to take from the public treasury $100,000 to cover all the expenses which may have incurred. I tell my friends on the other side of the House that there is a sleeping public sentiment North. I tell you, gentlemen, that you may carry on these acts, for there is no one here with power enough to prevent them; but you will be held responsible for all that has been done here. You are writing, by endorsing and ratifying the illegal acts of this Administration, one of the saddest, blackest pages in the history of this country (reference: *Congressional Globe*, Thirty-seventh Congress, First Session, July 24, 1861, page 224).

To learn more about war crimes, and other despicable acts of the Lincoln administration, I recommend people read the following books:

When in the Course of Human Events, by Charles Adams, a Northerner and a tax expert.

The Real Lincoln, by Thomas DiLorenzo.

The South Was Right, by Walter D. and James R. Kennedy.

Was Jefferson Davis Right? by Walter D. and James R. Kennedy.

Forced Into Glory: Abraham Lincoln's White Dream, by Lerone Bennett, Jr.

Those Dirty Rotten Taxes, by Charles Adams.

For Good and Evil, by Charles Adams.

CHAPTER ELEVEN
State's Rights and State's Sovereignty and State's Domestic Institution

◆ ◆ ◆

States' rights and State sovereignty was not something that I remember being taught about in my high school history book. States' rights and State sovereignty is backed up by the Ninth and Tenth Amendments of the U. S. Constitution. These two things, along with sovereignty, would have protected slavery for as long as people in the slave-holding States, North and South, wanted it to. But the main reasons for States' rights and State sovereignty were not just to protect slavery. It was (I believe) to keep the Federal Government in its proper balance. Where the Government overstepped its boundaries or misused and abused its authority, it could be put in check with States' rights and State sovereignty. This is something we the American people need to assert today. To assert something like this today would take real, strong-minded leaders who are willing to discharge their duties as leaders (Congressmen) to the Constitution faithfully and to the best of their abilities and not be influenced by special interest groups. It takes spiritually-minded people to withstand temptation.

For instance, let me use myself as an example: If I were a Senator who had the final vote on a bill and that bill was one where my vote could decide which groups of people would be a winner or loser of hundreds of millions of dollars, I know I would have to pray hard for spiritual wisdom, knowledge, and guidance because someone probably would try to tempt me with kickbacks of millions of dollars to vote their way. I admit it takes men and women who have guts to do the right thing. Sometimes we are faced with adversity, but decent people will find the power in themselves to do the right thing. Those are the kind of people we need to enforce the principles of States' rights and State sovereignty which Southerners died for, defending their homes, land, and territory from a tyrannical and evil U.S. Government.

At this moment I am going to briefly talk about the Civil War. It was not fought over slavery. States' rights and unfair tariffs (taxes) were the main reasons for that war. If anybody would read the Crittenden Resolution passed in July 1861, they would see that the U.S. Government (Senate and House of Representatives) affirmed that the war was to preserve the Union and not to end slavery. This should help to prove to people that if all Southerners wanted was slavery, all they had to do was to stay in the Union or stop fighting the war and rejoin the Union with all their rights (including the right to own slaves) unimpaired. You see, when the Federal Government was formed, it was intended to be the agent of the States and not their dictator. There was no question about the right of the States to secede, when they seceded from Great Britain and signed the Declaration of Independence. They signed it as thirteen free, sovereign, and independent States (not the United States, singular). When New York,

Virginia, and Rhode Island ratified the Constitution, they declared that if the Federal power became abusive and acted against their will, violating their rights, they had a right to secede from the Union and again resume their sovereign power to be free and independent nations among the nations of the earth. They made it very plain and explicit that States' rights and State sovereignty would be enforced by doing this. One of the ways I think the rights of States are undermined is by Federal mandates, coercion, or extortion. If you do not abide by their rules then they will withhold Federal money from your State. If this doesn't sound like a dictator, to some degree, instead of an agent of the States, then what does? What would happen if the people of Rhode Island voted not to pay Federal income taxes anymore? Please do not trouble your brain too much. I think I've got the answer. The despotic U.S. Government would send the American (or maybe United Nations) Armed Forces to make them pay. If you think this could not happen in this country, please think again.

I'm going to give an example of something that happened back in 1828 and 1832. It was called the Tariffs of Abomination. They were high, excessive, and abusive. South Carolina refused to pay those tariffs to the Federal Government. President Andrew Jackson responded by threatening to send Federal troops to make her pay those high taxes. South Carolina stood her ground. She used a process called nullification. It was either invented or endorsed by John C. Calhoun, who was a real Southern statesman and a strong leader. He resigned as Vice President of the United States over this issue. He was from South Carolina and he had the courage, determination, and mental strength to do what he thought was right.

These are virtues the government officials of our

time need today. Somebody might get mad at me, the writer, but sometimes making people mad is a by-product (side effect) of telling the truth.

Let me give an example of a States' rights and State sovereignty article that was published in the *Congressional Globe*, even though I disagree with it and I will explain why: This was taken directly from the appendix of the *Congressional Globe*, Thirty-seventh Congress, second session, page 227, left column:

> Mr. Speaker, there must of necessity be a supreme power in every nationality representing the public will. This political authority is called sovereignty. It is admitted by all that the whole people, properly represented in convention, may alter or abolish their present National Government and establish another; but the people of the several States can't do this, exercise this power.

I believe this part to be a lie. I believe this Congressman lied. The people and their representatives in free and independent States do have the
ish their relationship with their National Government when it becomes very abusive and passes laws that are harmful to their States. This is where knowing about the U. S. Constitution, States' rights, State sovereignty, and popular sovereignty comes in.

> They may change the several State constitutions and laws, with such limitations and restrictions as imposed by the National Constitution [I agree with this part]. They may make such alterations only and not change their relations to the General Government.

This second part I do not agree with. Remember, if the Federal Government becomes very intrusive and abusive, the people and their representatives in the sovereign capacity of their States have a right to alter and abolish their relationship with a tyrannical and evil government. Let me remind people that States' rights, State sovereignty, popular sovereignty (the will of the people), the Ninth Amendment, and the Tenth Amendment to the U.S. Constitution will back them up if they want to throw off, alter, or abolish their relationship to a tyrannical and evil government. But you must remember it takes strong leaders, like John C. Calhoun who gave up his position as Vice President of the United States because of the Tariffs of Abomination issue. I think to get a man of that caliber in this present time in politics is rare. Politicians must be reminded to do what they say – they will do it or else they will not be re-elected, period! No more scapegoating or lying should be accepted by the people of the United States. If you want a good, quality job done, get good, respectable, holy leaders to do it. A praying, devout Christian politician will have a very hard time getting elected because he or she can't be a master liar. But if we are to save our country from the destruction of the evil powers and moral decay, we had better pray and look hard to find them. Intestinal fortitude is what it takes to do the right thing.

Let me expound a little more about States' rights and State sovereignty. Those two principles really mean "home rule." Over one hundred years ago, people did not always see themselves as patriotic Americans first. A person was a patriotic citizen of their State first. Their allegiance went to the State first and to the United States second. This is what I think helps to give States' rights and State sovereignty more power. In the twentieth century people were brainwashed or conned with the Pledge of Allegiance to the flag of the United States of America. This may be very dangerous! First of all, we need to pledge our allegiance to serve the Lord Jesus Christ and do His will. Love and treat our neighbors with respect and dignity. Do some community service work when possible to help make our home area a better place in which to live. With people in all fifty States working together to better their States, this would be a better country. Would this kind of effort make it different? Yes, it would.

Getting back to States' rights and State sovereignty: Southern White people did not like a big Federal Government. They wanted home rule. They did not like outsiders telling them what to do. Real, diehard, devout Southern Confederate Americans do not like taking orders from Washington, D.C., that Yankee capital (not to be offensive). But that is the way they look at it. Especially the ones who know what the U.S. Constitution says have the guts to stand behind it. Strong States' rights and State sovereignty proponents might be the first people to get rounded up and put in concentration camps when the New World Order people put their programs into full effect.

People like myself who have some guts to speak out on things they believe in are better prepared to take whatever is dished out. We need to have a John C. Calhoun mentality. Principles, discipline, and morals come from having a good upbringing along with strong families and godly values. The moral core in our society has broken down. I believe this was something that had been intentionally done. Some people are sick and do not know it. That only makes things worse because they will not do anything about it. But most sensible people in their right minds will do something about being sick when they find out they are sick.

If you wonder why I'm talking like this, please stop and think. People who have a "say, do, or accept anything" attitude are no good to themselves or our society. That puts a burden on good, moral, respectable Christian people. But people who care about our world had better buckle up, get prayed up, and be stronger minded because from now on times are only going to get harder. Socialists and Communists are trained from their youth to their special purposes. They can tear down a country from the inside without firing a gun. Their way of doing things is creating social chaos and turmoil. They use males against females, Blacks against Whites, Jews against Gentiles, Northerners against Southerners, or whoever in order to accomplish their selfish goals. If you are wondering what this has to do with principles and morals, do not think too hard. I think I might have a solution. An unstable society can easily be taken over and destroyed, but a good, stable, moral Christian society could not be easily taken over or destroyed. It has to be conditioned over a period of decades to accept what was morally incorrect years ago (let us say over fifty years ago) as correct and proper today. I must admit that sin and immoral living will never be correct in God's eyes.

We must repent of our sins and evil deeds. We must rebuild our families. We must teach our youth how to be people of good character and dignity, to stand for what is right, and to speak out against what is wrong. When we do those things, hopefully, we will see a strong resurgence in States' rights and State sovereignty. Having good, healthy (mentally and physically) Christian people as citizens of your State will turn the country back in the right direction.

CONCLUSION

◆ ◆ ◆

In reading my book I hope that people would have a better understanding of slavery. I hope that some good will come out of me writing this book. It is not meant to defame the U. S. Government or anybody. It is written to tell the truth about slavery. Telling the truth might hurt people's feelings, but this kind of truth must be told, just like all truths need to be told all the time. We do not live in a perfect world. We live in a sinful world. People tell lies for their own benefit. Some people do not care who they hurt just as long as they are getting a paycheck. People who are reporters and history book writers need to report and write the truth. But having that kind of dignity and self-respect may not get them very far in their careers. So this is why it is more important for independent writers like myself to write the truth about whatever subject we are writing about. An independent writer can be truthful. When a person does not have a supervisor giving them instructions to lie, that is a plus – a plus for him and society.

The references in my book can be looked up on the Internet. Some references may be harder to find than others, but they can be found. The appendix to the *Congressional Globe* articles are on the Internet. Like any author, I want my book to be liked and respected. But most of all, I hope it is informative. I hope the information in my book will help make people's lives better. We need less hate and more love in this world. The topic of slavery needs to be talked about more out in the open. Blacks need to let go of hate, and White people need to let go of guilt. People need to stop being tricked, deceived, and lied to. The slavery issue needs to be studied more in depth and taught correctly in our colleges and high schools. May each and everyone who wants to know the truth about anything (including slavery), seek and search for the truth on their own. Do not depend on other people. They may be educated, but they may be an educated liar.

As I said, I hope that those who read this book have gotten a better understanding of American slavery. I hope they have gotten a deeper look at what has been hidden, kept a secret, or not taught to most American people about slavery. The truth is that slavery lasted 245 years under the American flag (including the American Revolution flag). When some people think of slavery they might think that it only existed in the South, but that is not true. Slavery existed in the beginning of this country in all thirteen free, independent and sovereign States. The Constitution of the United States was designed to protect slavery. The Federal Government protected slavery. The Supreme Court protected it. It was also protected by the American flag and international law (law of nations, laws of war) and treaties of the United States with foreign countries, Jay's Treaty being one of them. The Treaty of Ghent is another and the Treaty of Purchase of Louisiana is another that I can name. The reference for this is the *Congressional Globe*, Thirty-sixth Congress, Second Session, page 357, middle column, 1861.

Also, in the colonial era of this country, Newport, Rhode Island; Boston, Massachusetts; and New York City were this continent's major slave ports. A slave graveyard was found in New York City years ago. From the looks of the bones, trained experts could tell that the slaves were mistreated. Why don't special interest groups really jump on that bandwagon and demand that the truth be told about the history of New York City and other Northern history? Special interest groups have no problems when it comes to digging up dirt about Southern history. Somebody needs to remind people that Northerners sold their own slaves to Southerners. Northerners owned the slave ships. The banking, financing, the building of the slave ships, and slave expeditions was done in the North. The insurance part of this was all done in the North. Even Abraham Lincoln admitted that the North was just as responsible for slavery as the South. This is one time when I can say that he was being truthful instead of being a double-tongued hypocrite. He usually had one speech for the North and another one for the South.

POSTSCRIPT

◆ ◆ ◆

After reading the truth about the American flag, how do you feel? Did you, the reader, check out my references? Please do not be afraid to learn something new and to accept the truth. The truth is the light. The truth will set us free. Some people who say the Pledge of Allegiance to the American flag do not know what kind of flag they are saying it to. The American flag is a slave flag. It protected slavery. It flew on slave ships and flew over a slave nation for 245 years (ninety years as an independent Union of Free and Sovereign States). We all need to watch what we pledge our allegiance to. We all need to pledge our allegiance to Jesus Christ our Lord and Savior, to serve Him and do His will to the best of our abilities.

APPENDIX
Slave Clauses and Provisions in the U.S. Constitution
compiled by Dr. Robert Brock

◆   ◆   ◆

A. Article I, Section 9, Clause 1

The Migration or Importation of such Persons as any of the States now existing shall think or prefer to admit, shall not be prohibited by the Congress prior to the Year on thousand eight hundred and eight, but a tax or duty may be imposed on such Importation, not exceeding ten dollars for each Person.

In this clause, the Constitution provides for the increase of slavery by prohibiting the suppression of the slave trade for twenty years after its adoption. After 1808 it was left to the discretion of Congress to prohibit or not prohibit the African slave trade.

It was a deliberate criminal act on the part of the White people to continue to keep the Africans as captives and slaves after they have possession and ownership of said slaves and could have sent them to self-determination and freedom in Africa with reparations. By doing such, the United States became responsible for 169 years of

British slavery. The extension of this slave traffic in Africans to 1808 was voted for by the whole of the New England States, including Massachusetts, and opposed by Virginia and Delaware. The slave clause was inserted in the Constitution by the votes of the New England States. This clause of the Constitution was specially favored and protected by Article Five of the Constitution. We have seen that African slavery is increased through the slave clause in Article I, Section 9, Clause I, and now we turn to how the Constitution protects slavery impliedly by withholding all power to injure it or limit its duration, but protects it expressly by the following clauses:

B. Article IV, Section 2, Clause 3

No Person held to Service or Labor in one State, under the Laws thereof, escaping into another, shall, in Consequence of any Law or Regulation therein, be discharged from such Service or Labor, but shall be delivered up on Claim of the Party to whom such Service or Labor may be due (*Statutes at Large*, I., pp. 302-305: IX Stat. pp. 462-465).

C. Constitution, Article IV, Section 4

The United States shall protect... and on Application of the Legislature, or of the Executive (when the Legislature cannot be convened) against domestic Violence.

D. Constitution, Article I, Section 8, Clause 15

To provide for calling forth the Militia to execute the Laws of the Union, suppress insurrection and repel Invasions.

E. Provision: Constitution, Article V

...Provided that no Amendment which may be
made prior to the Year One Thousand Eight Hundred
and Eight shall in any Manner affect the first and fourth
fourth Clauses in the Ninth Section of the first Article....

Here again, the White people did a deliberate act
to cause and protect slavery by mutuality, even before
constitutional means, which is their admission of intention
to continue African slavery. Who prohibited Congress
from amending the Constitution? Who reserved and limited the Government and Congress in Amendment X?

F. Constitution: Article I, Section 9, Clause 4

No Capitation, or other direct tax, shall be laid,
unless in Proportion to the census or enumeration herein
before directed to be taken.

G. Constitution: Article I, Section 2, Clause 3

Representative and direct Taxes shall be appor-
tioned among the several States which may be included
within this Union, according to their respective Num-
bers, which shall be determined by adding to the Whole
Number of free [White] Persons, including those Bound
to Service [Free White People Providing Service by con-
tract] for a term of years, and excluding Indians not
taxed, three-fifths of all other Persons [Black African
Slaves – enumeration and political representation for
Master only].

BIBLIOGRAPHY

◆ ◆ ◆

Books and Articles

Finkleman, Paul, "Teaching Slavery in American Constitutional Law," *Akron Law Review*, Vol. XXXIV, Number 1 (2000).

Foote, Andrew H., *Africa and the American Flag* (New York: D. Appleton and Company, 1854).

Horne, Gerald, *The Deepest South: The United States, Brazil, and the African Slave Trade* (New York: New York University Press, 2000).

Lott, Stanley K., *Slavery and the U.S. Government* (Passaic, New Jersey: SKL Publications, 2005).

Lott, Stanley K., *The Truth About American Slavery* (Cartersville, Georgia: Eastern Digital Resources, 2004).

Lott, Stanley K., *Lincoln and the U.S. Government* (Cartersville, Georgia: Eastern Digital Resources, 2004).

Maltz, Earl M., *Slavery and the Supreme Court: 1825-1861* (Lawrence: University Press of Kansas, 2009).

Mundis, Jerrod, *Slave Ship: A Novel of Infamy* (New York: Wolf River Press, 2012).

United States Court Cases

Sylvia vs. Coryell, 1 Cranch, C.C. 32 (1801).

Scott vs. London, 7 U.S. 324 (1806).

Loughborough vs. Blake, 18 U.S. 317 (1820).

Cohen vs. Virginia, 19 U.S. 264 (1821).

North Carolina vs. Graham, 13 N.C. 263 (1830).

Johnson vs. Thompkins, 13 F.Cas. 840 (1832).

Hinds vs. Brazealle, 3 Miss. 837 (1838).
Moses Groves vs. Robert Slaughter, 40 U.S. 449 (1841).
Prigg vs. Pennsylvania, 41 U.S. 539 (1842).
Jones vs. Van Zandt, 46 U.S. 215 (1847).
Strader vs. Graham, 51 U.S. 82 (1850).
Norris vs. Crocker, 54 U.S. 429 (1851).
Rowan & Harris vs. Runnels, 53 U.S. 79 (1851).
Moore vs. People of the State of Ilinois, 55 U.S. 13 (1852).
Dred Scott vs. John F.A. Sandford, 60 U.S. 393 (1857).
Ableman vs. Booth, 62 U.S. 506 (1858).

Internet Resources

"The American Flag and the African Slave Trade" (March 19, 1860), New York *Times*; retrieved May 4, 2011, www.nytimes.com/1860/03/19/news/the-american-flag-and-the-african-slave-trade.htm.
"The United States and Spain Equally Responsible for the African Slave Trade" (December 8, 1860), New York *Times*; retrieved November 19, 2011, www.nytimes.com/1860/12/08/news/the-united-states-and-spain.html.

www.ingramcontent.com/pod-product-compliance
Lightning Source LLC
Chambersburg PA
CBHW061751020426
42331CB00006B/1432